Quiet Moments
for Grandmothers

Quiet Moments
for Grandmothers

Kay Marshall Strom

VINE
BOOKS

SERVANT PUBLICATIONS
ANN ARBOR, MICHIGAN

Vine Books is an imprint of Servant Publications especially designed to serve
evangelical Christians.

All Scripture quotations, unless indicated, are taken from the HOLY BIBLE,
NEW INTERNATIONAL VERSION®. Copyright ©1973, 1978, 1984 by
International Bible Society. Used by permission of Zondervan Publishing
House. All rights reserved.

Published by Servant Publications
P.O. Box 8617
Ann Arbor, Michigan 48107

Cover design: Paz Design Group

01 02 03 10 9 8 7 6 5 4 3 2

Printed in the United States of America
ISBN 1-56955-197-9

Library of Congress Cataloging-Publication-Data

Strom, Kay Marshall, 1943-
    Quiet Moments for granmothers / Kay Strom.
       p. cm.
    ISBN 1-56955-197-9 (alk. paper)
    1. Grandmothers—Prayer–books and devotions—English. I. Title.

BV4847 .S77 2001
242'.6431—dc21

00-047320

Dedication

I lovingly dedicate this book to my grandchildren, Phoenix, Sage, Moses, and Josiah, who are patiently teaching me what it means to be a grandmother, and to their parents Sara and Jim Ritchie, who are letting me learn on their children. In time I also plan to be grandmother to the children of Lisa and Arie Ringnalda, Toby Kline, and Eric Strom.

Introduction

J have a wonderful old Christmas photograph of little six-month-old me with my two grandmas. Grandma Marshall is holding me on her knee. Her hair is done up in a tight bun, she has on sensible laced black shoes, and her stockings are rolled up to her knees. Grandma Young is sitting in front of me dangling a Christmas ornament on which I am transfixed. She is wearing her gray hair in a matronly style, and her jersey dress is drab and shapeless. Two old women and a baby. Probably when the picture taking was over, my grandmas went back to baking cookies and knitting afghans, their main occupations.

"How old were my grandmas in this picture?" I asked my mother one day.

"Well, let's see," she said. She did a bit of figuring, then stated, "They were forty-five and fifty."

Forty-five and fifty? That wasn't possible! They were old women, and forty-five and fifty is just middle-aged!

Things sure have changed. Today's grandmothers come in all kinds. Some bake and knit, some go to the office every day, some play tennis and run in marathons. Some seem to do it all.

Some grandmas ease into their grandmotherhood in the old-fashioned way—they watch their children grow up and marry, then they eagerly await the birth of grandbabies. Others become instant grandmas when they marry men who have grandchildren. Many today see their children marry into ready-made families.

Some grandmothers are blessed to have their grandchildren close by, where they can be a part of their daily lives. More have to settle for grandparenting across the miles. An increasing number are closer and more involved than they ever dreamed of being—they are filling the role of mother, raising their grandchildren.

I have four grandchildren. Phoenix is seven and in first grade. Sage is five and will start kindergarten next fall. The twins, Moses and Josiah, are two. Grandmotherhood sort of crept up on me. I have known all four children since before they were born, and I have loved their mom for years. Two years after my first husband died, I married Dan, the children's grandfather.

The first time Phoenix called me Grandma Kay instead of just Kay, it caught me off guard.

Grandma! I hadn't thought of it that way before.

Grandma. What a nice thing to be.

Fellow grandmas, I want to invite you to step aside from your busy day—whatever that involves. Come away and let's have a quiet moment with the Lord.

A New Name

If my people, who are called by my name, will humble themselves and pray and seek my face and turn from their wicked ways, then will I hear from heaven and will forgive their sin and will heal their land.

2 CHRONICLES 7:14

I've been *Kay* my entire life—just plain Kay, not even short for Katherine. For thirty years I was *Mrs. Strom*. I was *Mommy* for several years, but not for long enough; way too soon my children were too sophisticated to call me by that childish name, and I moved on to *Mom*.

My daughter was married and my son away at school when my husband died after a long and devastating illness. For a while I wasn't sure who I was.

Then I married Dan, and I became *Mrs. Kline*—sort of. Actually, I didn't change my name, so I legally remained *Kay Marshall Strom*.

So many names. So many identities.

But along with Dan came something entirely new. Two months after we were married, his daughter Sara and her family were at our house for Easter dinner. As we relaxed together that afternoon, Sara's six-year-old daughter Phoenix casually noted, "You used to just be my friend, Kay, but now you're my grandma."

Grandma!

With this new name came a new role, and a whole new set of

honors, privileges, and responsibilities.

I remember hearing about a minister who insisted that the best prayer he ever heard was, "Lord, please make me the kind of person my dog thinks I am." Cute, but I'm not so sure about the theology. Anyway, I can top that prayer. Thanks to Phoenix, Sage, Moses, and Josiah, I now pray, "Lord, please make me the kind of person my grandchildren need me to be."

And I can best do that by making sure of my own true identity. It is being called by my Father's name—*Christian*.

Prayer for Today:
Dear Lord, may I always remember, in everything I do and say, whose name I bear.

Wishes for My Grandchildren

Pay attention and listen to the sayings of the wise; apply your heart to what I teach, for it is pleasing when you keep them in your heart and have all of them ready on your lips. So that your trust may be in the Lord, I teach you today ...

PROVERBS 22:17-19

I have always told my children that I fully intend to be a spoiling kind of grandmother. Part of the privilege and joy of being Grandma is being able to give recklessly. With my own children, I had to be sensible and practical. I always needed to keep my eyes focused on the long-term picture. I had to be concerned with setting a good precedent, because I carried the weight of my children's upbringing.

Not so with grandchildren. I can indulge their impractical whims. I can give them an extra-large slice of pie with ice cream even when they don't finish their broccoli. I can smile and take pictures as they romp and play in the garden and splash in the fountain on the patio, because I know that at the end of the day I can hand them back to their parents.

I want to be a fun grandma.

But love is not the only emotional message I am charged with giving my grandkids. With age comes some degree of wisdom, and wisdom brings deeper desires. Let me tell you some of the things I want to impart to my grandchildren.

I wish for them:

- The sense of accomplishment that comes from doing their best at something they never wanted to do in the first place.
- The willingness to pull themselves up after failure and to try again.
- The ability to entertain themselves when they are feeling bored.
- Taste buds that appreciate the delicious fresh things that grow in the garden.
- The wonderful pleasure of curling up under a quilt on a cold day and rereading a favorite book.
- A stirring of joy when they hear the old-fashioned hymns I sing to them.

Although I want my grandchildren to be successful, I don't wish them wealth or fame. I don't wish them beauty or eternal youth. Instead I wish them the wisdom that comes with time and experience. And I wish them a lifetime of enjoying the creation and knowing the Creator.

Prayer for Today:
Father, grant me wisdom to mingle fun and love with knowing God so that my little ones come to where they can "count it all joy."

A Little Child Shall Lead Them

His compassions never fail. They are new every morning; great is your faithfulness.

LAMENTATIONS 3:22-23

A few years ago, before I was remarried and gained my own grandchildren, I spent a wonderful Thanksgiving with my niece and her family. They live quite a distance away from me, and I'd had little contact with her three children. The youngest, four-year-old Christopher, I had never met.

When I arrived, I told the children I had gifts for them. Christopher knelt excitedly on the floor as I opened my suitcase. Teasing him, I pulled out my hairbrush and said, "Here, Christopher, this is for you!"

Imagine my surprise when he eagerly accepted the brush and said, "Thank you, Aunt Grandma! Thank you so much!"

I quickly retrieved the brush and gave him the truck I had brought him, and he squealed with delight.

But that first "thank you" made such an impression on me. How unusual to meet a child who is truly grateful for such an unexciting gift. As I lay in bed that night, I thought about my own thankfulness. Health, children, good friends, a comfortable home, a wonderful church family—all these were on my thankful list. But what about those more mundane things that I pretty much considered my just due? What about the "plain hairbrushes" in my life? There were so many I couldn't begin to count them all.

As I prepared to leave for the airport on Sunday evening, Christopher proudly presented me with a gift wrapped in his pillowcase. It was his toy action figure of Buzz Lightyear. "It's for you to play with on the airplane," he told me, "so you won't get wiggly."

I wanted to sneak Buzz back into Christopher's toy box, but my niece insisted he would feel bad if I didn't take his gift.

For the past two years, Buzz has stood on the mantle in my family room where I can see him every day. Each time I catch sight of him, I think of Christopher and the lesson in thankfulness he taught me.

Prayer for Today:
Thank you, Lord, for your great and everlasting faithfulness, especially in the little things of my life.

Who Matters Most?

Train a child in the way he should go, and when he is old he will not turn from it.

PROVERBS 22:6

I heard it again today: "I am a Christian because of my grandmother."

What's so unusual about that, you ask?

Nothing. That's the point. Many people know Christ because they saw his reflection in the lives of their grandmothers. That certainly was true for me.

We hear and read so much about what a tremendous influence other children have on our young ones. It's true to a degree. The problem is that we begin to believe their peers are all that matter to them. We wonder: *what possible lasting influence can we older folks have on young people today?* Many grandparents, like parents, shake their heads in dismay and say, "We make no difference at all!"

I just read about a recent study that is both interesting and heartening. The findings suggest that where prejudices and deeply held attitudes are concerned (and that definitely includes religious convictions!), friends actually have very little influence. And this study was done on teenagers! Peers, it seems, have more impact on a young person's *behavior* than on his or her *attitudes*. While the behavior may be distressing in the short run, in the long run it is the attitudes that determine who and what that child will be.

That may seem like little comfort to you if your grandchildren are acting irresponsibly. But don't give up. Continue to demonstrate your love in whatever ways you can. And without hitting them over the head with it, faithfully share your faith.

Let your grandchildren see the difference what you say you believe makes in your everyday life. For it's those deeply held attitudes that are going to carry your grandchildren through their lives.

<center>~~~~</center>

Prayer for Today:

Father God, show me when to act and when to love in silence. Help me to be faithful to never let a day go by without whispering a prayer for each of the young ones you have allowed into my life.

For Better or for Worse

And now these three remain: faith, hope and love. But the greatest of these is love.

1 CORINTHIANS 13:13

*N*ot long ago, I hardly gave a second glance to books or articles on grandparenting. Now I devour anything that has that magic word *grandmother* in it.

I was quite taken aback by an article written by a grandmother who described her twelve-year-old granddaughter as "a spoiled brat with a ring in her nose and not one decent thought in her head."

Hold it! Isn't the first requirement of grandmothering to love?

Usually, that's not hard. When little grandchild arms squeeze your neck, and little lips whisper, "I love you, Grandma," how can you feel anything but love? It's natural to love cuddly children who love us back. It's easy to hold our heads high when those little ones look up to us and show us affection, honor, and respect. It's easy to bubble over with happiness when they say sweet and affectionate things about us.

But what about grandchildren who want nothing to do with us? What about those whose words drip with sarcasm or ridicule or disrespect? What about those who insist we are so old and out-of-date we couldn't possibly have anything worthwhile to contribute to their lives? It's not so easy to love them.

God gave us the perfect model for love in 1 Corinthians 13.

But before you read it, let me warn you: it isn't necessarily going to say what you want it to say.

It takes a great love to be patient and kind to someone who is impatient and rude. ("All I want is a little respect! Is that too much to ask?")

It isn't human to not be self-seeking ("What *will* my friends say if they see her dressed like that?").

It isn't humanly realistic to not be angered, and when angered, to keep no record of wrongs ("What you *want* for your birthday? After the way you've been acting, I just might not get you anything!")

It takes a supernatural love to always protect, always trust, always hope, always persevere.

But love never fails. We have God's word on it!

***

Prayer for Today:
Lord, help me to model my love after yours.

No Longer a Child

When I was a child ... I thought like a child, I reasoned like a child.
When I became a man, I put childish ways behind me.

1 CORINTHIANS 13:11

*A*s I worked around the house, I sang:

> Our God reigns...,
> Our God re—e—i—igns,
> Our God re—igns,
> Our God reigns!*

That little praise song was in my mind, and I hummed and sang it on and off all day.

Four-year-old Sage was spending the day with me. He was inside and outside, running here and there. In the afternoon he busied himself in the family room making a town out of blocks. As he ran his little cars on the roads between the block buildings, I heard him singing softly. But what was he saying? I sneaked in closer so I could hear. He sang:

> God makes rain,
> God makes ra—ai—ain....

©1974, 1978 by L.E. Smith/New Jerusalem Music, P.O. Box 225, Clarksboro, N.J. 08020. Used by permission. Full five-verse version available on CD: Deep Calls to Deep.

I couldn't help giggling. Of course! It made perfect sense. Sage had taken my words and put them into something he could understand.

How nice it would be to understand like a child. How wonderful to look at God with such a simple focus. How great to put aside all the complex theological terms and debates and, with childlike faith, simply praise him for all the things we take for granted—things like the rain he showers on both the just and the unjust.

And that's the way God wants us to approach him—with a childlike faith.

Ah, but watch out. While Christ calls his people to become as children and to have a childlike faith, he does not intend for our faith to be *childish*. He desires us to grow and mature. And although we are never to lose the childlike faith, we are to put away childish things.

Prayer for Today:

Lord, help me to put away my childishness, but to keep my faith forever childlike.

All Men Are Created Equal

Blessed is the nation whose God is the Lord.

PSALM 33:12

The summer I was twelve years old, I was bored. Totally and thoroughly bored. I was tired of playing with my brothers and sisters, I was tired of doing jobs around the house, and I had read every kid's book in the house more times than I cared to count. In desperation I turned to the *Collier's Encyclopedia* on the second shelf in our living room. I had looked at the pictures in the twelve volumes many times, and I had often looked up various things. But I had never read it through from A to Z. So that was the project I set for myself that summer—read through the encyclopedia.

I read about aardvarks, bears, cannons, dikes, and many other things I have long since forgotten. But one thing I read I will never forget. It was the Declaration of Independence. It starts with these words:

"When in the Course of human events, it becomes necessary for one people to dissolve the political bands which have connected them with another and to assume among the powers of the earth..."

As I read, something magical happened. I was transfixed.

"We hold these truths to be self-evident, that all men are created equal, that they are endowed by their Creator with certain inalienable Rights, that among these are Life, Liberty, and the pursuit of Happiness...."

The words were so beautiful they brought tears to my eyes. When I finished reading it, I read it again. Then again, and again. Before the summer was over I had committed it to memory. To this day, the words of the Declaration of Independence move me to tears.

Your grandchildren likely have more books than they can read. They probably have computer games and television and videos and toys galore. But may I make a suggestion to you? Why not get a copy of the Declaration of Independence and read it to them. Tell them the story of those courageous forefathers—many of them great men of God—who forged such a magnificent foundation for our country.

Then pray with them for the United States of America.

Prayer for Today:
God of our fathers, thank you for the great blessings you have heaped on our country. May ours truly be a nation whose God is the Lord.

Long Term Thinking

"Love the Lord your God with all your heart and with all your soul and with all your mind."

MATTHEW 22:37

I am told that in Iroquois society, when leaders make decisions that affect their people, they are encouraged to remember seven generations in the past and to consider seven generations into the future. Wouldn't our country be a different place if our leaders would do more of that kind of long-term thinking?

I remember the wonder in my grandfather's voice as he told me, "My first trip across the United States was in a covered wagon. And look at me—I have lived to see space travel." Then, shaking his head, he added, "That's too long for anyone to live."

How fortunate we are as Christians! We can look far more than seven generations behind us. We can see how God rewarded the faith of our ancient forebears such as Joseph and Noah and Moses and Deborah. We can see his faithfulness to Isaiah and Hosea and Nehemiah. We can see how he worked through the fishermen in Galilee, in ordinary folk like Mary and Martha, and through such a rebellious persecutor as Saul of Tarsus—"the chief of sinners." We can look at the legacy left us by faithful Christians who met in the dark of the catacombs to worship, by Christians who stood firm in the face of persecution in China and Africa and all around the world.

As for the future, it is assured. We know how it all will end. It's right there in the back of the Book!

Grandchildren are such a blessing; they help us look backward, and they help us look forward. When we look backward and forward, it becomes much easier for us to understand where we should set our priorities. The very top priority should be to love God as he commands us to. If we do that, we can trust our past to him and rest assured that our future, and the future of those who come after us, is safely in his hands.

Prayer for Today:
Dear God, may I always and forever keep you as my number-one priority.

Actions Speak Louder Than Words

"Why do you talk so much when you know so little?"

JOB 38:2, CEV

Sometimes I am overcome with an unexplainable conviction that I am infused with great wisdom and insights. I look at others, and to me their behavior flaws seem so glaring. How can it be that they don't see those flaws themselves? Suddenly I am seized by the certainty that a straightforward, no-punches-pulled conversation with those persons will show them the errors of their ways. They will see the light and will forever be grateful that such a wise person as myself had sufficient kindness and courage to confront them. They will reform on the spot, and the world will be a better place because of my wise and candid guidance.

So I open my mouth.

Then reality hits. People are not so overjoyed to hear my opinions after all. They see no reason to turn from their actions to my way of doing things. They are completely unimpressed with my wisdom and insights. In fact, they don't appreciate my intrusion into their lives one bit.

Too often, we grandmas feel the necessity of imparting our wisdom to our grandchildren. We expect to reform them, and for our trouble to earn their everlasting gratitude. Instead, we find them rolling their eyes and denouncing us as hopelessly out of touch.

The best way to influence another person is not by the words we speak, but by the way we live. If we want our grandkids to be respectful, we need to be respectful to those around us—including to them. If we want them to be dependable, understanding, and compassionate, it is important that they see us being dependable, understanding, and compassionate. If we want them to be people of God, we need to model godliness before them. They need to hear us praying for the things and the people who are important to us—and that means them.

As the Apostle James says, "Look at my deeds and you will see my faith in action."

───────

Prayer for Today:
Dear Father, help me to ask for your guidance before I open my mouth. But in my daily life, help me to show the fruit of your Spirit—love, joy, peace, patience, kindness, goodness, faithfulness, gentleness, and self-control.

Sweeter Than Honey

Wisdom is sweet to your soul; if you find it, there is a future hope for you.

PROVERBS 24:14

*W*hen I first visited Margo, I was impressed by her home. She had so many gorgeous things. So many fragile treasures. And her carpets—they were thick, lush, and snow white. Then I saw the pictures of her grandchildren—two adolescent girls and four little boys.

"How do you keep your carpets so white with kids running in and out?" I exclaimed.

"Oh," she quickly answered, "I don't let my grandchildren in my house. When they visit, they stay in a hotel. I visit them there and we eat in restaurants."

What? Keep the children out so the carpet will stay nice?

That made me think. I do love keeping my house nice. And I am a strong proponent of teaching children appropriate behavior and respect for other people's property. But right then and there, in Margo's living room, I made some important resolutions. I decided:

- Food doesn't always have to be eaten at the kitchen table.
- Candles are for burning—even the cute ones shaped like flowers and animals.
- If pants don't look good in grass-stain green, they don't belong on children.

27

- It's more important to play with the kids than to get things crossed off my to-do list.
- If the crocodile story is worth telling once, it is worth telling 560 times.
- Children's books are meant to be read and reread until they fall apart.
- There is no bouquet as beautiful as hand-plucked wildflowers.
- Rose blossoms will grow back.
- Oatmeal chocolate chip cookies and a glass of milk make a well-balanced meal.
- Tomatoes from the garden are delicious even if they aren't quite ripe.
- Seeing the birds outside the window is well worth the cost of birdseed.
- Cats won't suffer permanent damage from having their tail spulled.
- If it's too valuable to be replaced, it belongs in a locked closet.
- People are far more valuable than things.

Clothes can be washed, floors can be mopped, dents and scratches can be covered up or ignored. But this day with your grandchild can never be replaced.

Prayer for Today:

Please, Father, give me the wisdom to let my grandchildren know nothing I own is more important to me than they are.

A Living Legacy

"These commandments that I give you today are to be upon your hearts. Impress them on your children. Talk about them when you sit at home and when you walk along the road, when you lie down and when you get up."

Deuteronomy 6:6-7

For several years I taught a class, Recollecting and Writing. I called it my "old people class." And it really was. Three-quarters of the people in it were born before 1910. I started off each week by assigning a specific topic ("My Favorite Toy," "My First Job," "The Scariest Thing That Ever Happened to Me," "My Best Prank.") We would all talk about the topic of the day, me asking questions and them reminiscing and sharing. During the week the class members would write on the subject, and the following week, for the last twenty minutes of class, I would read various submissions.

Oh, the experiences those people shared! Passive, weary, wrinkled faces broke into grins as they described the wonders they found under the Christmas tree when they were children. Tears ran down leathery cheeks as they told the horrors and losses of war and the ravages of long-forgotten diseases. And their voices softened and hushed as they told of the miracles that had touched their lives. In five years of teaching that class, I never had a person claim to not believe in God. Those folks had seen and experienced too much to be so arrogant and foolish.

The people in that class gave me a legacy of living history that I shall never forget.

Like those people who lived through so much, every Christian has a legacy to pass along. Sure, we have our own personal stories and family legacies, but we also have something much more important to preserve and pass on to future generations. We have a living, personal faith in a living, personal God.

It is indeed a blessing and a privilege to pass this legacy along.

It is also a serious responsibility.

Prayer for Today:

Lord, keep me faithful as I pass along the legacy that has come down from the patriarchs, was fulfilled in Jesus, and was passed on to me by so many men and women of God.

Lest We Forget

"Go over before the ark of the Lord your God into the middle of the Jordan. Each of you is to take up a stone on his shoulder ... to serve as a sign among you. In the future, when your children ask you, 'What do these stones mean?' tell them that the flow of the Jordan was cut off before the ark of the covenant of the Lord.... These stones are to be a memorial to the people of Israel forever."

JOSHUA 4:5-7

"What's that, Grandma?" Phoenix asked me.

"Oh, honey," I said, "I'm glad you asked!"

I sat down and took her on my lap. I told her about the fire that had destroyed my family's house. I told her how I had searched through the ashes, desperate to find something I could keep. It was so important to me to have something I could hold in my hands. But there was nothing left.

"I gave up and walked back through the ruins toward the street," I said. "But then I stumbled over something. I didn't know what it was, but I dug it out and blew off the ashes."

"Is that what you found?" Phoenix asked.

I reached up and took my honest-to-goodness, one-of-a-kind piece of modern sculpture off the shelf. Its base was formed by a set of turkey-shaped salt and pepper shakers, forever molded beak to beak by the crystal goblets that had melted over them. The turkeys had been a gift from Mrs. Eckert, my sixth-grade teacher who always had such faith in me and my potential. On top of them was the melted base of a silver candlestick, a wedding gift to me and Larry, my first husband, who at the time of the fire had already been showing signs of the disease that would later take his life. To one side were the melted remains of my grandmother's milk-glass sugar bowl, and on the other was a delicate china cup I got for my college graduation. Balanced on one side was my daughter Lisa's baby spoon and fork, and on the other was my son Eric's long-handled baby feeding spoon. The entire piece was cemented together and glazed over with a sparkling layer of melted crystal.

"This is my memorial stone," I told Phoenix. "God gave it to me to help me remember that he can take the worst tragedies of life and make something beautiful out of them."

It's God's job to provide. It's mine to remember and share.

Prayer for Today:

Place memorial stones in my life, dear Lord, lest I forget your faithfulness to me.

Lessons From Grandpa

Teach us to number our days aright, that we may gain a heart of wisdom.

PSALM 90:12

My Grandma Marshall told me many stories about my grandfather, whom I hardly remember. He was a farmer during the week, and he also ran a general store in the Ozark Mountains of Missouri. On Sundays, he was a circuit-riding preacher. From early in the morning until late at night, he rode a trail from one tiny town nestled in the hills to another hidden in a hollow to another tucked away beside a small stream.

"Oh, but them folks was glad for the day he was a-comin'!" Grandma told me with a big grin.

Everyone came to the church early to wait for Grandpa. They brought fried chicken and freshly baked pies, and they would sing and eat and listen to him preach way into the afternoon. No matter how long he stayed, they begged him to stay longer. They were poor folks, so they would pay him with whatever they had—chickens or freshly dug potatoes for instance, or maybe even a baby pig. One time my grandfather had come home dragging a load of freshly chopped firewood.

"That was pretty crummy pay for working all day!" I sniffed.

"Oh, no!" Grandma told me. "Them folks worked hard just to keep body and soul together. They gave your grandpa everything they had, just as if they was a-givin' it to Jesus hisself."

I wish I had known my Grandpa Marshall. I wish I had known those people in the hills and the hollows of the Ozark Mountains, too. They could have taught me a lot about praising God with psalms and spiritual songs, and about grace, and about a true hunger for God's Word.

My grandfather and those mountain folks could have taught me a lot about living my days aright, and so gaining a heart of wisdom.

⚜

Prayer for Today:

Teach me, Lord, the wisdom of making the most of every moment of every day you allow me on this earth.

Small Things

The Lord is gracious and compassionate, slow to anger and rich in love.

PSALM 145:8

In December 1999, when our calendars marked the end of the century and of the millennium, every magazine published lists of the most noteworthy people of the past and the wondrous things they accomplished. I read each listing I found and savored every account. Albert Einstein and Jonas Salk, Mahatmas Gandhi and Martin Luther King, Jr., Johannes Gutenberg and Winston Churchill, the Wright brothers and Thomas Edison—so many great people, so many exciting stories.

I love to hear stories of people who do wonderful things. I wish I could do great things that would positively change the course of history.

Although few of us will be listed among the greatest people of the century, in our own families we can accomplish great things. Making a commitment to pray every day for our children and grandchildren may not sound like much compared to developing a vaccine for polio, but, oh, what potential we may be unleashing in those young ones! Being available to listen to the thoughts and concerns of a grandchild may not sound very important when measured against making great decisions of state that affect the entire world. But, oh, how God can use our willingness to be available in the hearts of these leaders of the future. Being patient and loving and thoughtful and consistent—these don't sound like earthshaking accomplishments. Yet these are the very things that can help to shape the people who will shake up the world in the next century.

Mother Teresa once said, "We cannot do great things—only small things with great love."

Yes. That's it. It's not up to me to do great things. It is only up to me to be faithful and loving in the small things I'm given to do.

Prayer for Today:
Dear Lord, give me a heart of love and faithfulness for the small things you have for me to do.

Straight Paths

Trust in the Lord with all your heart and lean not on your understanding; in all your ways acknowledge him, and he will make your paths straight.

PROVERBS 3:5-6

*M*y friend Diane's first grandbaby was born four weeks early. Because baby Michelle was so tiny and suffering from jaundice, she needed to stay in the hospital for an extra two weeks. Diane's daughter Penny was released, but she was instructed to get plenty of rest, which meant not coming to the hospital more than once a day. Penny cried all the way home.

"I don't want my baby to be fed by strangers," Penny insisted.

"But they aren't just strangers," Diane said. "They are trained nurses who really care about the babies."

"But they don't *love* Michelle," Penny argued. "I want my baby to be held and fed by people who really love her. I want family there."

Diane called her husband, her other daughter, and her son-in-law's parents. Everyone came immediately. Penny's sister worked out a feeding schedule that included all of them. For the entire two weeks little Michelle was in the hospital, she was fed every meal cradled in the arms of a relative who really, really loved her.

I don't know how much difference it made to baby Michelle, but it certainly made a huge difference to Penny. She could rest and heal, comfortable in the knowledge that trusted, loving hands were caring for her infant.

Trust is a funny thing. It doesn't always make sense. But that's what makes it so wonderful. It doesn't *have* to make sense. We can trust even when we cannot understand. In fact, that is what we are instructed to do. If we trust in the One who knows and understands all things, he will be faithful to make our paths straight.

❦

Prayer for Today:

Lord, even when I am blinded by fear, despair, or discouragement, help me to trust you to make my paths straight.

It Is Well With My Soul

But he said to me, "My grace is sufficient for you, for my power is made perfect in weakness." Therefore I will boast all the more gladly about my weaknesses, so that Christ's power may rest on me.

2 CORINTHIANS 12:9

At the grocery store, I ran into a friend whose little grandson struggled with a chronic illness. I greeted her with, "Hi! How are you?"

"It is well with my soul!" she replied.

What a perfect answer to a mundane question.

In the fall of 1873, a businessman by the name of Horatio Spafford bid farewell to his wife and four daughters as they set sail for Europe. He planned to meet them over there after he finished some business arrangements in Chicago.

Several days later, at two o'clock in the morning, while the passengers slept and the captain guided the ship across a calm and gentle sea, it was suddenly rammed by an English vessel. The ship sank, taking 226 people to the bottom of the ocean. All four of the Spaffords' daughters were among those lost at sea. Nine days later, when the survivors finally made it to Cardiff, Wales, Mrs. Spafford cabled her husband: "Saved alone."

Immediately the grief-stricken father set sail to join his wife. In the middle of the night, when they passed the spot where the other ship went down, he poured out his grief to God. There at the ship's rail, out of his heartbreak and pain, Mr. Spafford wrote the hymn, "It Is Well With My Soul":

When peace like a river attendeth my way,
When sorrows like sea-billows roll,
Whatever my lot, Thou hast taught me to say,
It is well, it is well with my soul.

Throughout our lives things happen that we cannot understand. The timing hurts and baffles us. And yet, because God's
grace is sufficient and his power is made perfect in our weakness,
whatever the circumstances we can say, "It is well with my soul!"

Prayer for Today:
*Dear Lord, whatever my circumstances, help me to look
heavenward and say with confidence, "It is well with my soul!"*

❧

A Gift for Jesus

"If anyone gives even a cup of cold water to one of these little ones because he is my disciple, I tell you the truth, he will certainly not lose his reward."

MATTHEW 10:42

"How come I get presents on my birthday and I get presents on Jesus' birthday, too? Why don't we give presents to him on his birthday?"

Many parents and grandparents hear this question from their little ones. What a nice change it is from the more oft-heard demanding cries of "I want this!" and "Buy me that!"

Even if our young ones don't ask, we can make gift-giving time an opportunity to help them discover the joy that comes from giving something meaningful to another person.

But what about a gift for Jesus? What can little ones give in Jesus' name?

One seven-year-old girl promised to write a letter each month of the year to an elderly relative who lived many hours away from the rest of the family. This, she decided, would be her gift to Jesus. The first day of each month she brought out paper and pencil, along with crayons so that she could draw a picture to go along with the letter. Special days—Valentine's Day, Easter, Christmas, birthday—got special cards and pictures.

A brother and sister decided to go in together and earn money to sponsor a child through World Vision. Ten-year-old Julie wanted their sponsored child to be a girl from Africa, but eight-year-old David insisted on a boy from Honduras. So they sponsored Pablo. But the next Christmas Julie insisted they each sponsor a child. "That way we can each have who we want," she said, "and two kids can have food and go to school."

A teenager bought a cow through a mission program for a family in India. Another collected food for a homeless shelter.

But it isn't even Christmas yet, you say? No matter. This is the perfect time for you to come up with a gift of your own for Jesus. Share it with your grandchildren. Let them be a part of the joy and satisfaction you get from giving to Jesus by helping someone in his name.

***

Prayer for Today:
Help me, Dear Jesus, to give a gift to my grandchildren by letting them see me give to another in your name.

Pumpkins and Roses

My niece Melanie and her then four-year-old daughter Marie were visiting, and we were in the car on our way to dinner. From the backseat I heard a sweet little voice softly singing:

Go to sleep now my pumpkin
I will tuck in your toes.
If you sleep well my pumpkin,
You will turn to a rose.

I hadn't heard that song in years!

"Where did you learn that, Marie?" I asked.

"Mama sings it to me at night," she told me.

"My mother used to sing it to me when I was little," Melanie said.

It took me back to my childhood. My sister—Melanie's mother—and I would lie in bed, and my mother would sing "the pumpkin rose song" to us. "Where did you learn that song?" I once asked my mother.

"From my mother," she told me. "She used to sing it to me when she put me to bed at night."

Just imagine! That little song was once lovingly sung by

Marie's great-great-grandmother to her own little child!

I know something of the power of a song. Nothing can bring tears to the eye more quickly, or a wistful smile of remembrance, or a rolling laugh at the thought of a past event like a song with a history.

The psalmists of the Bible knew something about the power of a song. They challenge us to join with all of creation that can do nothing else but sing God's praises. The prophet Isaiah says it this way: "Shout for joy, O heavens; rejoice, O earth; burst into song, O mountains!"(Is 49:13).

Prayer for Today:

O God, may I never cease to shout for joy, to rejoice aloud, and to burst into song at unexpected times. And may every song—even the one about pumpkins turning to roses—lead me to you.

Instructions Included

"Ask and it will be given to you; seek and you will find; knock and the door will be opened to you."

MATTHEW 7:7

*E*arly on I let my children know that I intended to be a spoiling kind of grandma. I told them I reserved the rights to buy presents that are fun even though they are a complete waste of money, to bring my grandchildren worthless junk from any trips I take, and to fill their Christmas stockings and Easter baskets with yummy stuff that has no food value whatever. The frilly dresses and impractical shoes that I nixed for my own daughter are what I want to get for my grandchildren.

I know, I know. Spoiled kids can be a pain. But I maintain that there is a constructive type of spoiling that is actually good for children, and that no one can accomplish it as well as grandmothers. Constructive spoiling is founded on the twin principles of *love* and *respect*.

Few grandmothers need to be told to love their grandchildren. It comes naturally. But sometimes we do need to be reminded to respect the fact that Mom and Dad are the authorities over them. I have learned to ask Sara and Jim before I mention the candy box to the children and to first run my wonderful ideas for the kids past Mom and Dad.

Does God spoil his children? Absolutely! If you doubt it, just look at today's Scripture verse. But God also sets boundaries: he requires that his children walk by faith, and that they trust him

45

totally. (In Matthew 7:11, Jesus continues: "If you, then, though you are evil, know how to give good gifts to your children, how much more will your Father in heaven give good gifts to those who ask him!")

We can never love like God. Nor can we ever be as trustworthy to our little ones as he is to us. But we can look to him as a model of constructive spoiling.

That's why I let my grandchildren stay up past their bedtime and bounce on the waterbed and have just one more cookie.

Prayer for Today:

Holy Father, may I love my grandchildren with all that is within me. But may I demonstrate that love in a way that encourages and builds up the entire family.

The Pressure Cooker

But we have this treasure in jars of clay to show that this all-surpassing power is from God and not from us.

2 CORINTHIANS 4:7

*I*t was the end of summer, and in our kitchen canning was in full swing. We kids were busy slicing up piles and piles of apples. Grandma was making applesauce in the pressure cooker. After she finished with it, my mother seasoned it with generous amounts of cinnamon and nutmeg. Then she dished the hot, fragrant applesauce into glass jars, screwed on the tops, and set them aside to seal.

It was hard work, but, oh, how wonderful the kitchen smelled!

I vividly remember the hissing of the gauge on the pressure cooker top as it gently rocked. Now and then, when Grandma and Mom were especially busy, the pressure built up and the hiss grew more insistent. We were finishing up our last batch of applesauce when the insistent hiss suddenly became a shriek. With a frightening bang, the top blew off the pressure cooker. The kitchen walls and ceiling were covered with applesauce.

Our pressure cooker was a heavy, sturdy pot, shiny silver inside and out. It cooked all kinds of delicious things, yet as far as I know it only blew its top that one time.

Why didn't the apostle Paul describe me as a pressure cooker? Generally speaking, I look pretty good. I am sturdy and useful, and I can take a good bit of pressure without blowing up. Sure, I sometimes hiss fairly loudly, but I do pretty well.

But Paul doesn't write about pressure cookers. He talks about clay jars.

In Paul's day, clay jars were ordinary and everyday. They had little value and even less beauty. As vessels, they certainly couldn't stand up against much. Drop them and they would break into a hundred pieces.

But something made those jars of clay special. It was what was inside them. Because they weren't showy and didn't call attention to themselves, they were perfect places to hide precious treasures.

Ah, that's the picture. I may like to think of myself as a self-sufficient pressure cooker who can take a great deal before I blow. But what I really am is a simple clay jar, valuable beyond measure because of the treasure that is within me.

That takes the pressure off!

Prayer for Today:
Dear God, take me, a simple jar of clay, and fill me with a treasure beyond value.

Forgive Us Our Debts

Be kind and compassionate to one another, forgiving each other, just as in Christ God forgave you.

EPHESIANS 4:32

orgiveness is not a human attribute. If you doubt this, spend time with a group of small children. You will hear something like this:

"He hit me first!"

"It's not my fault!"

"That's my toy and I want it!"

"No, *I* want it!"

"You're mean! I hate you!"

If you hear anything about forgiveness, it will likely be from the frustrated adults who are urging the little ones, "Please, *please*, play nice!"

No, forgiveness is not the human way.

But it is God's way.

Actually, forgiveness studies are an increasingly hot topic among medical doctors today. More and more magazine articles and books expound on something that has become known as "forgiveness therapy." We are coming to understand that holding a grudge, nursing anger, and harboring resentments can indeed affect our health. In fact, it has been suggested that refusing to forgive contributes to everything from high blood pressure to heart problems to cancer.

Said one doctor at a public symposium: "It might be that you will actually live longer, feel happier, and suffer less pain if you simply say—and really mean—these three words: 'I forgive you.'"

The interesting thing was that the doctor presented this as an entirely new, cutting-edge idea. Wrong! Two thousand years ago, Jesus told us the way to live: we are to forgive one another.

We are to model the divine attribute of forgiveness for all the world to see. It is to be our way of life.

***

Prayer for Today:
Thank you, dear Lord, for the gift of forgiveness you offer me. Help me to be quick to forgive others in your name.

Living Letters

You yourselves are our letter, written on our hearts, known and read by everybody.

2 CORINTHIANS 3:2

*W*hether your grandchildren live on the next block or on the other side of the world, writing letters can be a wonderful way for you to let them know they are always in your heart and on your mind. Here's an idea: look through your calendar and think of a special letter to write each child, each month of the year. For instance:

- *January:* The beginning of a new year is a wonderful time to reflect on what God has done during the past year, and to anticipate what he will do in the coming year. "Last year God gave you a new baby brother. And in this new year you will be starting kindergarten!"
- *February:* What could be a better time than Valentine's Day for a message about God's love?
- *March:* Spring flowers, baby animals, new life. This month is especially good for a letter with pictures.
- *April:* A "Happy Easter" letter might be decorated with chickens and bunnies and lambs and eggs.
- *May:* Did you know that the National Day of Prayer occurs in May? Let your grandchildren know you are praying for them this month. And share with them a prayer God has answered for you.

- *June:* There would be no Mother's Day or Father's Day if it weren't for kids! How about a Children's Day letter?
- *July:* Write a letter telling why you are grateful to God for this country.

You are already over halfway through the year. By now, your grandchild will be eagerly anticipating your monthly letter. You may even be getting some letters in return!

Prayer for Today:
Dear Lord, may every letter I write speak of the One whose message is written on my heart. May it be pleasing to you as it is known and read by everyone with whom I come in contact.

Beauty From a Jumble

For you created my inmost being; you knit me together in my mother's womb. I praise you because I am fearfully and wonderfully made; your works are wonderful, I know that full well.

PSALM 139:13-14

J remember going to my friend Lorraine's house and watching her grandmother busily working on a large piece of dark cloth. She was weaving a jumble of brightly colored threads into it. I was fascinated. It looked nothing like my grandmother's knitting with perfectly formed stitches in nice, even rows.

After watching her for a while I told Lorraine, "Your grandmother sure does messy work."

"It'll turn out pretty," Lorraine assured me. "You just have to wait."

After weeks of watching the fabric become more and more jumbled and confused, I put the question straight to Lorraine's grandmother: "Is it *ever* going to look like something?"

"Oh, yes," she said. She turned the cloth over and there before me was a beautifully detailed scene of snowy mountains above and trees, grass, and beautifully colored flowers below. Soft white clouds floated through the clear blue sky. And over in the corner, peeking out from behind an aspen tree, was an intricate doe with huge brown eyes.

I ran my fingers over the tiny stitches that fit together so perfectly. "It's beautiful!" I said.

"The backside is where I do the work," Lorraine's grandmother told me. "But this is the real side. This is what I'll hang on the wall."

So often when we look at God's handiwork in the people around us—ourselves included!—what we see is the jumbled backside. We shake our heads and sigh, "What a failure. Nothing good can ever come out of this."

Oh, but there is that other side. When we see it, we will gasp at the beauty and perfection we find. That's the real side, the one that will be on display for all eternity.

***

Prayer for Today:
Almighty God, please take the jumble of threads that is my life and weave them together into a beautiful tapestry that will cause others to exclaim, "What a wonderful God she serves!"

A Lone Tree in the Desert

"My Father will honor the one who serves me."

*I*n several communities in England, children without grandmothers will soon be able to have publicly funded substitutes. Mothers with small children who don't have close relatives to help them out can apply for "community grandmothers." The program is being touted as "rent-a-granny."

How will it work out? Only time will tell. Some insist it will be like re-creating an extended family. Others fear the scheme will simply create an army of government-sponsored babysitters.

It is an interesting concept, though. And on a less organized, non-government-sponsored or subsidized basis, the idea has been around for years. Long before I was a bona fide grandmother, I was an acting grandma to children in our church congregation. I volunteered to babysit when their parents needed a night—or even a weekend—away but were too strapped for money to hire someone. I bought stickers and lollipops by the bushel to sneak into welcoming little hands. I sent birthday cards and valentines and Christmas cards.

The Talmud says: "A mother is likened to a mountain spring that nourishes the tree at the root. But one who mothers another's child is likened unto a water that rises into a cloud and goes a long distance to nourish a lone tree in the desert."

The same can be said for grandmothers. Sure, we are a busy bunch, but we have experience and energy, and we have enough love to share.

Take some time to look beyond your own grandchildren. Do you see any lone trees in the desert who need to be nourished? Can you give a mom a break by offering an afternoon or evening of loving child care? Can you send a special card saying "I love you" to a little one who doesn't have a grandma nearby? Can you buy or make or bake a special surprise for that little one and deliver it with a hug?

"In as much as you do it to one of the least of these," Jesus tells us, "you do it unto me."

⚬⚬⚬

Prayer for Today:

Help me, Lord, to make room in my life for a little one who is like a lone tree in the desert. Give me a heart like yours—a heart of love.

The Gift of Tradition

The boundary lines have fallen for me in pleasant places; surely I have a delightful inheritance.

PSALM 16:6

*C*hristmas of 1983 came at the end of a yearlong bleak stretch for my family. My husband had been out of work for a year. We had long since gone through our financial reserves. We had even cashed in our life insurance policies. Basically we were living on what we grew in our little garden and the eggs from our chickens. But I had set aside twenty dollars for Christmas.

I began my shopping at a secondhand store; everyone got a "new" outfit. Next came the drugstore, where I got a personal grooming item and a favorite candy bar for each stocking. As I left the store, I looked at the bills and change I had left in my hand. Not much. This was going to be a lean Christmas.

Then I got an idea. Our public library sells donated and withdrawn books for a very reasonable price. I spent the rest of my money there. When I got home, I got out the leftover Christmas wrapping paper from the year before and wrapped each item and book separately. The children were delighted when they got home from school and saw the pile of presents under our crooked little tree.

Christmas morning came, and it was a greater success than I could have hoped. Lisa, who had just started junior high school, and Eric, who was in fifth grade, loved their assortment of books. We all spent a good part of the afternoon reading.

The books were such a success that the children wanted me to shop at the library again the next year. I did, and I have done so every year since. Withdrawn library books for Christmas have become a cherished tradition in our family.

This year I also shopped for withdrawn books for my grandchildren. I got hardback board books for the little boys, picture books for Sage, and easy readers for Phoenix. In this Christmas gift, my grandchildren got more than an assortment of books to enjoy. They got the gift of tradition.

Prayer for Today:
Thank you, Father God, for my great inheritance. And thank you for the Book that tells me all the facets of it.

More Than I've Asked

"Moreover, I will give you what you have not asked for—both riches and honor—so that in your lifetime you will have no equal among kings."

1 KINGS 3:13

*M*y grandchildren's eighty-nine-year-old great-grand-mother was in the hospital where she had been taken after she suffered a mild stroke at her home. We were pleased with her progress and her determination to regain the use of her left leg and arm.

After several days, Sara brought the two older children to the hospital to see "GG," who has played such an active and important part in their lives. Phoenix and Sage walked quietly into the hospital room. They went over to the bed and kissed their great-grandmother. After quietly surveying the room, Sage fixed his eyes on the woman in the bed and asked, "GG, when are you going to have your baby?"

No one laughed harder than GG.

"Imagine!" she said. "A baby at eighty-nine! Wouldn't that be something to write home about?"

It would indeed! That is a blessing most of us would prefer not to imagine. Even those of us who drive sporty cars and run around town in warm-up suits and stay in shape by playing ten-nis and taking aerobics classes. Even those of us who hold down full-time jobs or are back in school as students. Even those of us who almost feel we are actually getting younger rather than older. Even for us, motherhood is no longer in our life plans.

Of course, none of us really know how our lives will play out. God alone knows that. But we do know that by giving us children, grandchildren, and great-grandchildren, he has laden us with riches and honor we never even knew to ask for. And he has let us see it in our lifetime.

•••

Prayer for Today:

Dear Father, thank you for giving me more than I could ever dare to ask. Help me to recognize the riches and honor you have given me in my grandchildren.

Shelter in the Time of Storm

For in the day of trouble he will keep me safe in his dwelling; he will hide me in the shelter of his tabernacle and set me high upon a rock.

PSALM 27:5

It was a stormy day, and I was eating lunch with the class of fifth-graders in their classroom. The children pulled their desks together into various groups. Several girls were whispering and giggling. A large group of kids was trading jokes. Three boys were canvassing the room, looking for someone willing to trade cookies for apples. Everyone was talking and laughing. All except Jennifer, that is. She was eating alone in a back corner.

"Come on up with the rest of us, Jennifer," I invited.

"Oh, I can't," she said quickly.

"Why not?"

"Because," she said, "I stink."

I had substituted at this same school for several years, and I was well aware of poor Jennifer's predicament. She had been taunted and teased since kindergarten. Since she didn't protest, the taunting had grown progressively worse. Now, it seemed, even she believed it.

That was fifteen years ago. Last week I ran into Jennifer in the grocery store, and she looked wonderful.

"What are you doing now?" I asked her.

"I'm a teacher in a small town up north, and I love it," she said. Then she added, "It's funny, but it's just like my grandmother used to tell me. When all the kids used to make fun of me, I would come home crying that I hated school. My grandmother always said that someday I would be a teacher myself, and that things would be different in my classroom. And you know what? They are. I don't allow the kids to pick on one another."

Jennifer had had a defender in her grandmother.

Now she is a defender of others.

***

Prayer for Today:
Thank you for being my eternal defender. In the day of trouble, thank you for keeping me safe.

Put a Guard on My Mouth

When words are many, sin is not absent, but he who holds his tongue is wise.

PROVERBS 10:19

*H*ow we anticipate those first words from a baby's mouth. "Did you hear that?" we exclaim eagerly at the first babblings. "He said GaGa! That means Grandma. He's so tiny and he said Grandma!"

Soon the babbling becomes real words with less questionable meanings—words like "No!" And from then on, words pour forth.

Researchers give us various estimates as to the number of words an average person speaks in a day. But on one thing they agree—it is a lot. One researcher says a good average is thirty thousand words per day. That's enough to fill a small book! Drawn out into a lifetime, one person's words could actually fill an entire library.

Some of that multitude of words are good and positive and helpful and uplifting. Many, however, are not. If you are anything like me, you wouldn't be very eager to have a library containing the sum total of your words read by anyone.

We think about being good stewards of our money and of our time. But did you ever think about being a good steward of your words?

Here is my own personal paraphrase of Philippians 4:8:

Finally, sisters, whatever is true, whatever is noble, whatever is right, whatever is pure, whatever is lovely, whatever is admirable—if anything is excellent or if anything is praiseworthy—those are the things you should be talking about.

The gift of speech is one of God's great blessings to us. And as with his other blessings, we will most certainly be held accountable for what we do with it.

___

Prayer for Today:

Dear Lord, you said that out of the overflow of my heart my mouth speaks. Keep my heart clean and pure so that my words will be a blessing to all who hear them.

Strength for Today

I can do everything through him who gives me strength.

PHILIPPIANS 4:13

*G*reg's grandmother doesn't see him anymore.

She spends a lot of her time sitting in her living room, staring at the faded spots on the wall where pictures used to hang. Until recently those walls were filled with pictures of Greg. Now they are empty.

"I had to take his pictures down," she says. "It upset me too much to see that sweet little face smiling at me, knowing that I can't see him or talk to him."

Greg's parents are divorced. His father has disappeared from his life, and his mother has remarried.

"His mother told me that since my son walked out of Gregory's life, it is best for the boy if I stay out of his life, too. I do want what's best for him. But I just can't believe that taking a loving person away from a hurting child is best."

There are times when, despite our tears and our best efforts, we cannot have things the way we are certain they should be. Some grandmothers have to stay outside their grandchildren's lives despite their longing to be let in.

In these days of divorce and remarriage and blended families, the problem is becoming more and more common. Even the United States Supreme Court is hearing cases of what rights grandparents legally have.

Most grandparents choose not to pursue such a matter through the courts. They don't have the money to do so, and they don't want to add to the child's trauma by being pulled in yet another direction.

If you are, or if you know, such a grandmother, remember this: the time will come when that child will be an adult and will be able to make his own decisions about seeing you. Prepare now for that time. Save pictures you would like for him to see. Keep a journal of things you would like to share with her. If you can send letters and cards, do so regularly. Pray daily for the child. And don't forget to pray for yourself as well. Ask God to give you the strength to be the very best grandmother you can possibly be in spite of the circumstances.

Prayer for Today:

Dear God, give me the strength to do what I must do. Give me patience and wisdom as I wait upon your timing.

Lessons in Life

Choose my instruction instead of silver, knowledge rather than choice gold, for wisdom is more precious than rubies, and nothing you desire can compare with her.

PROVERBS 8:10-11

A number of people of varying ages were asked this question: *What is the most important thing you've learned in life?* Here is a sampling of the responses.

- I've learned you can't hide a piece of broccoli in a glass of milk (age 7).
- I've learned that just when I get my room the way I like it, Mom makes me clean it up (age 13).
- I've learned that silent company is often more healing than words of advice (age 24).
- I've learned that wherever I go, the world's worst drivers have followed me there (age 29).
- I've learned that if someone says something unkind about me, I must live in such a way that no one will believe it (age 39).
- I've learned that children and grandparents are natural allies (age 47).
- I've learned that keeping a vegetable garden is worth a medicine cabinet full of pills (age 52).
- I've learned that making a living is not the same thing as making a life (age 58).

- I've learned that life sometimes gives you a second chance (age 62).
- I've learned that it pays to believe in miracles. And to tell the truth, I've seen several of them (age 73).

Some pretty good homespun philosophy there. But what I like best of all is what the Apostle Paul shares with us in Philippians 4:11-12:

- Whatever my circumstances, I have learned to be content (age 50+).

Now there is a life lesson worth learning!

⚬⚬⚬⚬⚬

Prayer for Today:
Dear Lord, I pray that you will give me the peace and joy that come with contentment despite my circumstances.

Lessons by the Piece

Why are you downcast, O my soul? Why so disturbed within me? Put your hope in God, for I will yet praise him, my Savior and my God.

PSALM 43:5

On my wedding day, I received a very special gift from my grandmother. It was a quilt she had made, pieced together in the Double Wedding Ring pattern. That in itself made it a nice gift, but there was something extra special about that quilt. It was made from scraps saved through the years from my clothes. As I looked around the pieced circles, I exclaimed, "Hey, here's that navy blue dress with the white clovers I wore in fifth grade!" and, "Look, it's the lavender print of the first skirt I ever made for myself!" and, "My yellow Easter dress! I always felt so beautiful in that."

The pieces of fabric in that quilt represented all the years—and experience and memories—of my childhood. The wedding rings pattern represented my hopes and plans for my future as an adult. And the circles? Why, they are an emblem of eternity.

Oh, there was something else about that quilt. There was a mistake sewn into one corner—a piece that didn't fit correctly into the block. My grandmother had put it in intentionally.

"Why?" I asked her.

"It's to keep the person who made the quilt humble," she told me. "You can't be proud of something that has such a mistake."

It is important that we allow ourselves to remember the past, both the good and the bad. If we don't remember, we don't learn from it.

It is important that we live in the present. This is where God has us; right here, right now, for such a time as this.

It is important that we live for eternity. All of this life is really just a preparation. We know that our existence will go on and on. And in its perspective, our past and our present take on a whole new light.

And wherever our life leads, we need to walk humbly.

Prayer for Today:
O God, you are always the same. O you who change not, abide with me.

Leave the Choice Up to God

God does not show favoritism.

*W*hen I look at two-year-old Moses and Josiah, I am amazed at how alike they are. My husband swears that their little faces and bodies are identical. Even their voices sound alike.

But they are two different people. Josiah talks more than Moses. And he is attracted to our tiger-striped cat as yellow jackets are attracted to a picnic; he just cannot keep his hands off her. Moses is the one who can throw a ball perfectly straight. He could do that since he was a year old. While both boys head straight for the fountain on the patio on the south side of the house, on the north side, Josiah goes right for the tomatoes that grow in my garden while Moses can't resist the wild strawberries that meander along the garden wall.

In some ways, all children are alike. Yet each one is different, even the most identical of twins.

I have always been mystified by the biblical stories of families who were convinced that they knew best what their children should be and took it upon themselves to make certain it happened their way. Rebekah is a good example—or should I say, a bad example. She had twin sons, Jacob and Esau. Early on she chose Jacob as her favorite, while her husband Isaac chose Esau.

It so happens that Jacob was the one God chose to follow in the patriarchal line of Abraham and Isaac, but God was well able to establish this line without Rebekah's interference. Because she could not trust God and his timing, she rushed in to encourage her favorite son to deceive his father and cheat Esau out of his inheritance. Her interference caused pain and suffering for the family that tainted its relationships for generations to come.

God chooses each of us to fill a specific role in life. No one, not even a twin, can fill that role as well as the person God ordained. Why can we not trust him to show each person his or her proper role?

~

Prayer for Today:
Dear God, take away my earthly tendency to play favorites and make choices that are not mine to make.

Go With God

The Lord is my helper; I will not be afraid. What can man do to me?
HEBREWS 13:6

*A*ngela has been living with her grandmother Eleanor for several years now. Just last week Eleanor and her husband won legal custody of their eight-year-old granddaughter.

"I love my daughter," Eleanor says with a sigh, "but I will never understand why she acts as she does. She is rough with poor Angie, but even worse, she has boyfriends in who treat the girl terribly, and my daughter does nothing to protect her."

Angie's grandparents have been looking out for her for most of her young life. They would always take her on a moment's notice ("My daughter has been known to literally drop her on my doorstep") and keep her until her mother would reappear to claim the child. Finally Eleanor could take no more.

"I always promised I wouldn't interfere with my daughter's parenting decisions," Eleanor says. "I always said I would just stand by to give my support when it was needed. But the time came when I had to fight for Angie. Goodness knows she couldn't fight for herself."

It isn't always enough to stand by and offer loving support. Today, more grandparents than ever have to step in to raise their grandchildren. In fact, chances are you know of someone who is doing exactly that. Perhaps that someone is even you.

"The Lord is my helper...."

Eleanor is learning what it means to truly claim the Lord as her helper. Although the judge immediately agreed that Angela needed to be away from her abusive home, the girl's mother is furious. "She calls me and tells me she will get back at me for stealing her child. I try to stay calm and tell her she can come and see Angela whenever she wants to."

"I will not be afraid...."

Without a doubt, going through the legal system is a last-resort action. But if it is necessary for the child's physical or emotional safety, go with God.

"What can man do to me?"

Exactly.

Prayer for Today:

Thank you, Almighty God, that you are in ultimate control. Take away my fear as I look to you as my great helper.

Sins of My Youth

Remember not the sins of my youth, nor my transgressions: according to thy mercy remember thou me for thy goodness' sake, O Lord.

PSALM 25:7, KJV

"Tell me stories about when you were little. Tell me about when you were my age."

I used to ask that of my grandparents, and my grandchildren ask it of me.

I tell the children about my childhood adventures and misadventures. I tell them about all the pets I had—including the opossum and raccoon and the goat. I tell them about the places I played—including the forbidden boarded-up house—and the trouble I got into.

Within reason, that is. To be perfectly honest, there are things I don't tell them about. There are things I don't even want to remember myself.

What will I do when the children are older adolescents, say, or even worse, teenagers? How will I respond when they ask me, "Did anything like this ever happen to you, Grandma?" What will I say if they ask, "What is the stupidest thing you ever did?"

Would I be a better or a worse grandmother if I gave them a full accounting of my own mistakes and sins?

We can take a clue from David. He sinned grievously, but he repented of those sins, imploring and receiving God's forgiveness. He doesn't deny his sins and foolish actions, but he doesn't dwell on them either. In the Psalms, he puts far more emphasis on praise to God, and on God's great forgiveness.

We do not have to disclose everything about our past in order to be good grandparents. But it is important that we allow our grandchildren to see that we are fallible humans. It is important that they know that we, like them, are in need of God's forgiveness. Otherwise, how will they understand that his forgiveness is sufficient for them just as it is for us?

Prayer for Today:
Thank you, O Lord, for removing my sins from me as far as the east is from the west. Thank you for remembering them no more. Help me to show your mercy to those who transgress against me.

Rewind!

It is God who works in you to will and to act according to his good purpose. Do everything without complaining or arguing, so that you may become blameless and pure, children of God without fault in a crooked and depraved generation, in which you shine like stars in the universe.

PHILIPPIANS 2:13-15

Sage was too busy playing to join Phoenix and me to hear the story of my kitten Twinkle who was given away when I was a child and then walked across the Golden Gate bridge and all through the city of San Francisco to get back home again. Just as I was getting to the exciting part—Twinkle was stealing a fish at Fisherman's Wharf—Sage decided he wanted to hear the story after all. He ran over and climbed up on my lap. But he didn't just want to join in where we were. He wanted to go back and hear the part he had missed.

"Rewind, Grandma, rewind!" he insisted.

Modern technology! How times have changed.

Yet how kids remain the same. Sometimes impatient. Sometimes insistent. Sometimes demanding. Sometimes determined.

What a good opportunity to allow us to let God work within us to will and to act in his good purpose. What a perfect chance to practice the virtues of doing what we need to do without complaining or arguing.

No, it isn't easy. And I really can't describe any of us as

blameless and pure—certainly not myself. Yet as children of God we can stand securely and confidently in his presence. When we do that, we can insert our name on these lines:

You, *(your name)*, may become blameless and pure, a child of God without fault in a crooked and depraved generation, in which you, *(your name)*, shine like stars in the universe.

***

Prayer for Today:
Make me, O Lord, blameless and pure in your sight. Cause me to shine like the stars in the universe.

A Tale of Two Sons

If any of you lacks wisdom, he should ask God, who gives generously to all without finding fault.

JAMES 1:5

Donna and Will have two sons. Brian is the "good" son. He works in the family business, has a wife and three children, and they all enjoy one another. Paul is the "other" son. Shortly after he was married, he and his new wife borrowed money from Donna and Will for a business venture, "just until we get our feet on the ground." The business went all right, but it wasn't the big money earner they had hoped it would be. And what with one thing and another, they just never seemed to feel as though their feet were really on the ground, and the money was never paid back.

"They took advantage of us," Donna says. "We were nothing but a bank to them."

"They could well afford to help us out," Paul says. "Why do they have to be so stingy with their own family?"

Although Paul and his wife and their four children live less than thirty miles away from Donna and Will, the children have never seen their grandparents. They have never even spoken to them on the telephone. And with each passing day, it seems less likely that they ever will.

"I would love to have things different between us," Donna says. "Some days I just sit by the phone waiting for my son to call and apologize. I long for him to include us in something his family is doing."

Will that ever happen?

Probably not.

Words said cannot be unsaid. Deeds done can never be undone. And if you sit and wait for an apology, you will likely wait forever.

For all of us, there comes a time when we need to humbly ask God for wisdom as we ask ourselves: *What is really important here? Who all is suffering because of my determination to do this my way? How much is it costing me emotionally to maintain my stubborn pride?*

Stop waiting for a change. You make that change happen.

Prayer for Today:
Holy Father, I know I lack wisdom in the words I speak and the deeds I do. Please, please, give it to me generously.

Use Me!

Surely the arm of the Lord is not too short to save, nor his ear too dull to hear.

ISAIAH 59:1

I love to hear stories about people who overcame handi-caps and obstacles to achieve something truly worth-while. I'm inspired by Thomas Edison, whose early teachers gave up on him for being too dull to learn. I'm moved by Helen Keller, who overcame the seemingly insurmountable obstacles of complete blindness and deafness to achieve so much. And Walt Disney: did you know he was once fired from a newspaper because he had a "lack of ideas"? Joni Eareckson Tada, who was left paralyzed from the neck down by a diving accident, has moved and ministered to untold thousands with her painting, singing, speaking, and writing.

Just imagine!

And what of Moses? God chose him to lead the Israelites out of Egypt and into the Promised Land, yet he insisted he wasn't capable of such a task.

"No one will believe that you sent me!" Moses argued.

So God gave him three miraculous signs to prove God was with him: the ability to turn his shepherd's staff into a snake and back again, to turn his hand leprous and then clean, and to turn the waters of the life-giving Nile River into blood. Who could doubt that God was behind powerful signs like these?

"But I can't speak right!" Moses insisted. "I can't approach

Pharaoh if I can't talk!"

God pointed out that he himself was the Creator. He had made Moses, and he would provide him with the words he needed to accomplish his task.

Even so, Moses pleaded, "Please, God, send someone else to do this."

God sent him. And God used a doubting, stammering man with nothing in his hand but a stick to change the course of history.

Is God asking you to do something that you don't feel qualified to do?

Never, ever, underestimate God!

~

Prayer for Today:
Please, dear Lord, help me never to hinder your work by insisting "it can't be done." Thank you, Father, that you alone are sufficient.

Beeping Hearts

May the words of my mouth and the meditation of my heart be pleasing in your sight, O Lord, my Rock and my Redeemer.

PSALM 19:14

When Josiah and Moses were born two months early, they were the tiniest babies I'd ever seen. After weeks in the hospital, they were finally allowed to come home, where their big sister and brother were eagerly awaiting them. But both little boys had to be hooked up to monitors and checked frequently.

Sara tucked the babies into side-by-side dresser drawers that served as perfectly sized baby cribs.

"Yep," three-year-old Sage announced as he proudly showed us his new brothers, "their hearts are beeping!"

When it comes to spiritual matters, I definitely want my heart to be beeping. When God speaks, I want to be attuned to hear his voice. And I want to realize that he always hears me—every joyful word I speak, every question I ask, every broken-hearted tear I cry.

I want God to know me as I really am.

In their book *Walk the Talk*, Eric Harvey and Alexander Lucia write: "We judge others by their actions. We judge our-selves by their intentions." How true that is! How often do we reason—or even say!—"This is what I believe, but, well, the situation is different for me, because..."? We can come up with rationalizations and justifications for just about anything.

But God sees through all that. He doesn't merely listen to our words and our reasonings, but he sees the intentions and motivations behind them. Nothing is hidden from him. We have no secrets from God.

When God sees the things I do and hears the words I speak, and when he sees the hidden thoughts and longings of my heart, I want him to be pleased.

***

Prayer for Today:
Dear Lord, may no word come from my mouth, or thought or intention come from my heart, that is not acceptable to you.

A Gift for You

We have different gifts, according to the grace given us.

ROMANS 12:6

*M*y Dear Grandchildren:

I went outside to cut a bouquet from my rose garden this morning, and I couldn't help thinking of all of you. That pink rosebush in front has so many full, fluffy blossoms. Behind it are the creamy white ones that stand so tall and regal. Some blossoms are huge and some are quite small. Some, like the deep red ones that look like velvet, have a wonderful perfume, but others, like the yellow ones, have hardly any fragrance at all.

There must be some more of those caterpillars you found the other day, because I see leaves that have been nibbled, especially the dark green ones near the back. Those leaves must be especially sweet and tender.

Some of the blossoms are fading, and their petals are drooping. But there are also a lot of buds. Some are hard and green, not even close to opening.

I had to step back and look at my roses all growing there together in the brick planter. So many colors; all so beautiful. And, oh, their wonderfully sweet fragrance!

In the end, I didn't cut any. I couldn't. With any of them gone, the rose garden just wouldn't be the same. Every single bloom—even the faded ones and the buds, and every single leaf—even the ones the caterpillars had chewed—had its place.

Each one contributed to the beauty of the whole.

That rose garden made me think of you, Phoenix and Sage and Moses and Josiah. Each one of you is so wonderful in your own way. Each of you is beautiful and oh, so sweet. Each of you has something special to contribute, and without any one of you, life would not be right.

I want to thank each of you for the beauty you have brought into my life.

And here is a promise I make to you: I want to help you to find your place to bloom.

With much love,
Grandma Kay

Prayer for Today:
Help me to see the specialness of each of these little ones you have brought into my life. Allow me the wisdom to help them to bloom where they are planted.

From the Master's Hand

God has arranged the parts in the body, every one of them, just as he wanted them to be.

1 CORINTHIANS 12:18

*A*ntonio Stradivari was an Italian maker of musical instruments. During his long career, he made well over one thousand violins, cellos, and other instruments. In each of his handmade masterpieces he put a label inscribed with the Latin version of his name: *Stradivarius*. Today, more than two hundred years after his death, the name *Stradivarius* is still synonymous with suburb excellence.

Every human being is a masterpiece handmade by God. Each one of us is created in his image. And that's not all; if we are followers of his Son, Jesus Christ, we are also stamped with his label: *Christian*.

Yesterday we talked about the uniqueness of each of our grandchildren, and how without any one of them the garden of our lives could not be complete. But sometimes it is easier for us to see the touch of the Master in the little ones around us than it is to see it in ourselves.

Our society has stamped its idea of worth on us: beauty, wealth, accomplishments, the trappings of success. We hold ourselves up against all that and we feel worthless.

But how could that be? Worthless, when we bear the label of the master Creator? Impossible!

God has made us just as he wants us to be, bumbles and

stumbles and warts and all. He has put us in the place and time that he, in his great wisdom, knew was best. Without you and without me the body of Christ is not complete.

Forget about longing to be what you aren't. Instead, look for a way to fill the spot that no one else can fill as well as you.

Prayer for Today:
Thank you for making me in your holy image. Help me to know the part of the body you created me to be.

Recycled Mama

"If you remain silent at this time, relief and deliverance for the Jews will arise from another place, but you and your father's family will perish. And who knows but that you have come to royal position for such a time as this?"

ESTHER 4:14

"For me, the *grand* has been taken out of grandmother," says Cynthia. She has been raising her three grandchildren, now all teenagers, since they were babies. "I don't get the luxury of spoiling them and then sending them back to Mother. I *am* Mother."

This is not the way Cynthia had imagined spending her autumn years. "My husband and I talked about all we would do after retirement—travel, sleep late, visit with friends, pick up and go whenever and wherever we wanted. Instead I'm back to early mornings, birthday parties, homework, and PTA meetings."

Things often don't work out the way we plan. Esther knew all about that. She never wanted to be a captive in Persia. She never asked to be entered into the beauty contest the king was running. And when she won, she quickly discovered that being queen wasn't all it was cracked up to be. The welfare of the entire Jewish people depended on her approaching the king and making a request. Trouble was, going before him without being summoned could easily mean she would be killed.

What a predicament!

It was her cousin Mordecai who put it to her straight: "God can accomplish this without you, Esther. But who knows? Maybe he put you here just for such a time as this."

God could provide for Cynthia's grandchildren without her. But who knows? Maybe he put her exactly where she was just for the purpose of raising them.

How about you? Maybe God put you exactly where you are for a very special reason, too. Perhaps there is no one on earth who can do that job as well as you.

Maybe you are here just for such a time as this.

Prayer for Today:
Thank you, dear Lord, for choosing just the right time and place for me. Thank you for such a time as this.

Yours, Mine, Ours

But you are a shield around me, O Lord; you bestow glory on me and lift up my head.

PSALM 3:3

On Mother's Day my husband Dan announced he was taking his favorite moms to dinner. There were four of us: Dan, me, his daughter Sara, and his first wife's mother, Margaret.

When the waiter came over he said, "Hi! Are you all a family?" We answered together, "Yes!"

That family group could also have included my first husband's mother, Clara, whom I am still close to; my mother; my daughter Lisa; and Sara's mother-in-law, Judy. We are truly a family of the time!

Today, blended families are a fact of life. Although it can be a confusing fact, it can also be beneficial. With its changing cast of adults and children, the blended family has been called the contemporary version of the traditional extended family of a past era.

My grandmother used to look at me and say, "Honey Child, I can see myself in your eyes." When I look at my grandchildren, I see nothing of myself in them. Yet I have had the privilege of knowing Phoenix, Sage, Moses, and Josiah since they were born, so it hasn't been difficult for me to create a connection with them. I know something of their desires and their fears, their preferences and their weaknesses. I know better than to mention a sleepover unless we can do it today. I know not to have more pieces of candy out than it's OK to eat. I know we should keep our distance from the gorilla compound at the zoo, and we shouldn't even think about going near the clock with the moving eyes at the airport.

Most of us would prefer that our families stay stable. The old and familiar is more comfortable than the new and unknown.

But nothing in life stays the same.

Perhaps more than ever before, we need to ask God to grow a hedge of protection around our changing families.

~

Prayer for Today:
O Lord, be a shield around me. Father God, lift up my head.

Lord of the Future

"For I know the plans I have for you," declares the Lord, "plans to prosper you and not to harm you, plans to give you hope and a future."

JEREMIAH 29:11

*Y*ou know what I'm thankful for? Not knowing the future. There are so many things I would have vexed and worried about had I known what was coming in the next day or month or year. Yet all my anxiety and worrying would not have changed one single thing.

Unfortunately, I do my share of worrying anyway. And I know I am not alone in this. Just look at all the anxiety and hand-wringing that went into anticipating the turn of the calendar from 1999 to 2000. I think our grandchildren and great-grandchildren will be amused and mystified by that!

Good things and bad things will happen to each of us, and also to our friends and families. No matter how much we long to protect our loved ones from pain and disappointment, we cannot. But what we can do is keep our eyes firmly fixed on the almighty God who carries the future in the palm of his hand. Our children and grandchildren and great-grandchildren will see us living out the certainty that we don't need to know where we are going so long as we know who is leading the way. By our faith, we can be a living object lesson to those around us.

In the waning days of December 1999, I heard this statement on the radio: "Get a grip on the God who holds the future, and you can let go of the stress."

Actually, that is pretty good advice for any century.

We don't know the future (thank God).

But God does know it. In fact, he *is* the future!

Prayer for Today:
You are Lord of the past, Lord of the present, and Lord of the future. Thank you that your ways are the best ways, and your paths the right paths.

Lasting Treasure

Provide purses for yourselves that will not wear out, a treasure in heaven that will not be exhausted, where no thief comes near and no moth destroys. For where your treasure is, there your heart will be also.

LUKE 12:33-34

*W*hen I was growing up, there was no money in our family for anything fancy or luxurious. *Practical*—that was our motto. When I was in high school, my best friend gave me a pair of silk underwear for Christmas. Soft and smooth, and decorated with the most exquisite lace, it was far too nice to just wear. But I was starting college the next fall. I would wear it then.

I took my beautiful silk underwear to college with me, but it was too lovely to wear on anything but the most special occasions, so it stayed safely stored in the back of my dresser drawer.

The summer after I graduated from college, I was married. Certainly my wedding would be the perfect time to wear my silk treasure. But then again, maybe not. I saved it for my honeymoon. But no day seemed to be the right day, so I kept it packed in my suitcase.

When our house burned almost twenty-five years later, my beautiful silk underwear—still wrapped in the tissue paper it had come in—was destroyed. I had never once worn it. Oh, I had thought about it many times. I had looked at it and touched the soft silk and exquisite lace trimming. But I had saved it and saved it until it was too late.

I made a decision after the fire. Never again was I going to own anything that was too nice to use. Never again was I going to wait and wait until just the right time and the most perfect of circumstances. It was time to begin living life to its fullest.

We have a strange idea of where our treasures lie, don't we? We think it has to do with belongings and bank accounts and investments. But when we get it stored up, moths come in and begin to nibble away at it. Rust takes over and it crumbles away. Thieves break in and steal it. Or fire burns it up, or the stock market plunges and wipes it out.

The only treasure we have that will stand the test of time is the treasure we store up in heaven. And there with the treasure will be our hearts.

***

Prayer for Today:
Help me, Lord, to worry less about my earthly treasure and concern myself more with the eternal treasure I am storing up in heaven.

Picked Just for You

*Lord, you have assigned me my portion and my cup; you have
made my lot secure.*

PSALM 16:5

*P*hoenix and Sage came in from the hillside with their
hands clutching clumps of dandelions and wild sour
grass. Fresh dirt clung to the roots, which were still attached.
The sour grass was already beginning to droop and wilt.

I looked up from the fistfuls of weeds at the two beaming
children who were presenting them to me. "We picked these
pretty flowers just for you!" they exclaimed with excitement and
pride.

Never have I gone out and picked a bouquet of dandelions
and sour grass for the kitchen table, but I'll have to tell you, the
one presented me that day was truly beautiful. What made the
difference? The golden flowers? No. They were always out
there. The eager little faces smiling up at me? No. Phoenix and
Sage were generally eager about something or other.

The difference was *me*. I had been coaxed into seeing the
beauty I usually overlooked and into appreciating the excitement that generally evades me.

It reminded me of my friend Maggie, who is a first-grade
schoolteacher. One morning she was reading a story, her class
sitting around her on the floor. The sun streamed in the window and across the chair in which she sat.

"Teacher," one little girl said, "do you have a kitten?"

"No," said Maggie. "Why do you ask?"

"Because," said the child, "you have kitty scratches on your cheek."

Perplexed, Maggie looked at her face in a mirror. Those "kitty scratches" were fine wrinkles!

Maggie told me, "That moment I decided I no longer had wrinkles. What I had was kitty scratches!"

And that day in the kitchen, as I got a crystal vase for the dandelion and sour grass, I decided there were no weeds in my yard. Only pretty flowers.

***

Prayer for Today:
Lord, help me to see the lot you have assigned me through your eyes, and to thank you for it.

Ravens and Lilies

"Consider the ravens: They do not sow or reap, they have no store-room or barn; yet God feeds them. And how much more valuable you are than birds!... Consider how the lilies grow. They do not labor or spin. Yet I tell you, not even Solomon in all his splendor was dressed like one of these."

LUKE 12:24, 27

I was teaching third grade in a large elementary school. One morning all of us teachers were called to the teachers' room for an emergency meeting. We hurried over, leaving our classes unsupervised. We were all worried about leaving the children alone, but Mrs. Whiting was more concerned than any of the rest of us. Her class of first graders was especially mischievous and unruly.

When we got to the teachers' room, Mrs. Whiting said, "I think I had better listen in and find out what's going on in my classroom." She went to the intercom and turned it on. Sure enough, her room was in chaos. We could hear children yelling and jumping and throwing things. But one little voice shrieked out over all the rest of the uproar.

Mrs. Whiting recognized the piercing voice at once. She picked up the microphone and in her sternest voice said, "Elizabeth, sit down!"

Immediately the room fell silent.

After a few seconds, a tiny voice answered meekly, "OK, God."

We teachers knew all about intercoms and microphones, but little Elizabeth, from her perspective, could think of only one explanation for a voice that came out of nowhere and admonished her by name.

When things happen to us that we can't understand, we try desperately to make sense of them. We affix meanings and consequences. "It's all my fault," we say. Or, "It's someone else's fault that this happened to me." Or, "God just doesn't care about me." If we can't make some sense of it, we give up in despair, certain that God has forgotten us.

We are like little Elizabeth. Our grasp of things is far too inadequate; our perspective is far too limited. We need to take time to stop and consider the ravens that fly in the air and the lilies that bloom in the fields.

But the time will come when we will understand. When that happens, we will certainly say, "Thank you, God. I wouldn't have it any other way."

Prayer for Today:
Dear Lord, help me to trust you until the time when I can see from your perspective.

The Family of God

The body is a unit, though it is made up of many parts; and though all its parts are many, they form one body.

1 CORINTHIANS 12:12

When I was in college, I attended a church with a fairly large group of college students. On the first Sunday of the school year, during the group's orientation, the pastor told us the benefits of being involved with an entire church family.

"There are some people I especially want you to meet," the pastor said. "You will be better college students for knowing them. First, Mildred Anderson."

Mildred struggled to her feet, and stood leaning on a cane. To my young eyes, she looked to be about 110 years old.

"Next, little Tanesha."

Tanesha stood on her chair so we could see her. She was a curly-headed three-year-old.

"And Bill Johns."

He was a balding middle-aged plumber.

The pastor introduced several more diverse people, and we kids looked questioningly at each other. What in the world could any of these people possibly have to do with us?

But all those people made it their job to get to know us. They went out of their way to talk to us. They invited us over for dinner and hired us to babysit for their children. They made sure we were personally invited to various church and community activities.

As the school year went on, we began to see that all these people did indeed have something to do with us. We learned from each of them. In them we saw life in action. We learned lessons in wisdom and patience. We learned tolerance and hope. We learned to look at things through different eyes and to hear through other ears.

And I learned a very special lesson. I learned that it is vital to never isolate myself into a safe-feeling group limited to people like me.

We learn from each other.

***

Prayer for Today:
Help me, dear Lord, to learn from every person you put into my life. And help me to live in such a way that they can learn from me as well.

Making Families God's Way

But when the time had fully come, God sent his Son, born of a woman, born under law, to redeem those under law, that we might receive the full rights of sons. Because you are sons, God sent the Spirit of his Son into our hearts, the Spirit who calls out, "Abba, Father." So you are no longer a slave, but a son; and since you are a son, God has made you also an heir.

GALATIANS 4:4-7

*I*t was the first day of school, and Mrs. Martin, the sixth-grade teacher, was getting acquainted with the students in her class. When Tom and Stephen Jamison introduced themselves as brothers, Mrs. Martin could barely hide her amazement. Stephen, tall and thin, had sandy-blond hair and a freckle-covered face. Tom was short and husky with a headful of unruly black curls.

"Surely you boys aren't twins!" Mrs. Martin exclaimed.

"Oh, no," Stephen replied. "I'm five months older than Tom."

"Yeah," Tom agreed. Then he added, "One of us is adopted, but I forget which one."

The boys' casual attitude toward adoption made such an impression on their teacher that she decided to make it a point to meet their parents and see for herself what kind of a family could foster such open-minded acceptance in their children.

When Mrs. Jamison visited her sons' classroom later that week, Mrs. Martin greeted her warmly. "I can't tell you how impressed I am with your boys!" she exclaimed. "It's wonderful to see a family in which adoption makes no difference at all."

"I'm afraid you don't understand," Mrs. Jamison said quickly. "Adoption makes a great deal of difference in our family. In fact, it has been a regular part of our conversation since our sons were toddlers. You see, we are all adopted—my husband and me and Stephen and Tom—all of us." Noticing the teacher's puzzled look, Mrs. Jamison explained, "We are Christians. Each of us has been adopted by God into his family. So now we're all his children. It's God himself who is the model for our attitude toward adoption."

As adopted sons and daughters, all Christians are truly the children of God.

❦

Prayer for Today:
Thank you, dear Lord, for adopting me into your family. Help me to live like a child of the King.

Help From Above

"Take my yoke upon you and learn from me, for I am gentle and humble in heart, and you will find rest for your souls."

MATTHEW 11:29

*L*ittle Katie was walking along the beach with her father when she spied a beautiful rock wedged in the surf. It glinted in the sun, crystal sparkles shining out from the dark stone. "I'm going to get that rock and take it to Grandma for her rock garden," Katie said. She dashed over to the rock and started to tug at it. She pulled and she pushed, but she could not get it to budge.

Her father walked up to her and said, "Katie, you're not using all the strength you have to pick up that rock."

"Yes, I am, Daddy," Katie said.

She struggled some more, grunting and groaning with the effort, until she was worn out. "Stupid rock!" she exclaimed as she stomped off in frustration.

"Katie," her father called out, "you didn't use all the strength you have to pick up that rock."

"Yes I did!" Katie insisted. "And it's too hard. I couldn't do it."

"No, dear," her father said, "you didn't use all the strength you have, because you didn't ask me to help you."

I don't know about you, but I can be an awful lot like Katie. I rush up to a challenge and insist, "I can do it! I can do it all by myself! Just watch me!" Then when I fail, I cry out, "Oh, what's the use? I did the best I could, but it's just too hard.

It cannot be done."

The truth is that, through Christ, we have immeasurable strength and power at our disposal. We are not using everything we have unless we have finally given up our prideful determination to do it all by ourselves and agreed to look to God for help. When we do that, it is amazing how much we can accomplish.

And there is a bonus. It is there, working together in the same yoke, that we finally find rest for our souls.

Prayer for Today:
Let me work together with you in your yoke, dear Father. Grant me your strength and your rest.

A Precious Proverb

He who cherishes understanding prospers.

PROVERBS 19:8

A second-grade teacher gave the children in her class the first part of several old proverbs, then asked them to fill in the rest. Look at our collective wisdom when seen through the eyes of children:

- It's always darkest before ... *daylight saving time.*
- Never underestimate the power of ... *termites.*
- You can lead a horse to water, but ... *how?*
- A Miss is as good as a ... *Mr.*
- You can't teach an old dog new ... *math.*
- A penny saved is ... *not much.*
- Don't put off until tomorrow what ... *you put on to go to bed.*
- Laugh and the whole world laughs with you, cry and ... *you have to blow your nose.*
- None are so blind as ... *Helen Keller.*
- Children should be seen and not ... *spanked or grounded.*
- There is no fool like ... *Aunt Edie.*

In the book of Proverbs, we find wonderful guideposts that can help us along as we make our journey through life. But that's just what proverbs are—guideposts. They are not specific promises. Unless we understand this, we can make an awful lot of assumptions that make perfect sense to us, but are as far off the mark as the thoughts of these second graders.

When you read the book of Proverbs, ask God to give you the understanding to apply each one properly and wisely to your life. And take that understanding, hold it to you, and cherish it. You will be wiser because of it.

Prayer for Today:

Dear God, I don't just want to know, I want to understand. Grant me your wisdom.

The Last Shall Be First

"But many who are first will be last, and the last first."

*G*randma was making breakfast for her grandsons, five-year-old Matthew and three-year-old Brian.

"I want the first pancake!" Matthew announced.

"You always get the first," Brian protested. "This time I want the first!"

As the boys argued, Grandma saw a chance to teach them a lesson in Christian living. So she said, "If Jesus was sitting here at the breakfast table, he would say, 'Let my brother have the first pancake. I can wait.'"

For a moment there was silence. Good, Grandma thought with a satisfied smile. My words are sinking in.

Then Matthew turned to his younger brother and said, "Brian, you be Jesus!"

Sounds a bit like Jesus' own disciples, doesn't it? Remember brothers James and John who took Jesus aside to try to work out a deal so that they could spend all of eternity sitting on either side of him? Jesus answered with strong words about those who push for a high position that will give them an advantage over others. Jesus told the disciples something that must have sounded mighty strange to them. "Whoever wants to become great among you must be your servant, and whoever wants to be first must be slave of all" (Mk 10:43-44).

I don't suppose James and John much cared for that approach. We don't like it much, either. Our human nature cries out, "Me first! Take care of number one! If I don't watch out for me, who will?"

But think of this: When would you rather have your turn at being first? Here on earth in the pancake line? Or in heaven, for all eternity?

***

Prayer for Today:
Help me, O Lord, to be willing to be the last and the least. Help me to be willing to be the servant.

Green Tomatoes

Wait for the Lord; be strong and take heart and wait for the Lord.
PSALM 27:14

hoenix and Sage were outside the kitchen door in my garden. Although many of the tomatoes were large and round, they were still shiny green. A few had pink blushes where they were just beginning to ripen.

"Can we eat some tomatoes?" Sage asked.

"They aren't ripe yet," I explained. "When they turn red, they will be juicy and sweet. But now they are hard and sour."

"But what if we find a red one?" Sage said. "Then can we eat it?"

"There aren't any ripe ones yet," I said. "We'll have to wait."

"But if we *do* find a red one," Sage persisted, "then can we eat it?"

Yes, I agreed, if they found a red one they could eat it.

A little while later I looked out the window. Phoenix and Sage had their hands full of green tomatoes. One look at their faces told me that the tomatoes were indeed still unripe and very, very sour. How much more delicious the sweet ripe tomatoes would be, but the children just couldn't wait.

I know how they felt. There are things in my life that seem so important that I just have to have them now. Sure, I might have warning signs that it isn't God's perfect timing, but I just can't wait. The more I look at that thing, the more I think about it, the more convinced I am that I have to make it happen *now*.

Remember Rebekah in the Bible and her twin sons Jacob and Esau? Jacob was her favorite, and it just happened that he was also the one God had chosen to follow in father Isaac's line, even though Esau was older and Isaac's favorite. Rebekah was well aware of God's choice of Jacob. But she couldn't wait for God's timing. She had to take matters into her own hands. At her urging and with her help, Jacob tricked his old, blind father into giving him the inheritance and blessing due Esau. Rebekah paid dearly for the deception. Her darling Jacob had to run away to escape his brother's fury, and she never saw him again.

How much better it is to wait until the tomatoes are ripe!

Prayer for Today:
Teach me to wait, dear Lord, teach me to wait.

To-Do List

Be strong in the Lord and in his mighty power.

Ephesians 6:10

$\mathcal{T}$hinking he was about to die in a plane crash in 1983, America Online executive Ted Leonsis started making a list of 101 things he would do if he survived. The plane landed safely, but that list changed his life. So far Leonsis has crossed off nearly two-thirds of the things he listed, including catching a foul ball at a baseball game and owning a sports team (he became majority owner of the National Hockey League's Washington Capitals in 1999).

I am not on an airplane in danger of going down, but the fact is that my life is moving on at an incredible speed. When I got up this morning and caught a glimpse of myself in the mirror, I was shocked. I am well aware that I'm getting older—but that woman in the mirror? She couldn't be me! Yet seeing her there staring back at me started me thinking about making my own list of 101 things. So far I am up to number 34.

My list is not nearly exciting enough to include catching a foul ball or owning a sports team. In fact, some of the items on it are downright dull (grow spinach in my garden all year round). Others are more interesting (successfully growing an orchid). Some are challenging (visiting Christians in isolated places of the world and recording their stories). Still others have to do with making my time on earth of more lasting value to those around me (helping to finance a brick-making machine for an energetic congregation in Africa).

What accomplishments are important enough to make your list of 101 most important things you want to accomplish during your lifetime? Do you have relationships that need to be repaired? Books you want to read? Gifts you want to give? Poetry you want to write? Spiritual goals you want to achieve?

Why not start your list today? Don't wait until the plane you are on is going down!

Prayer for Today:

Help me, Lord, to set wise goals for myself. And grant me the perseverance to achieve them.

Forward, Not Backward

One thing I do: Forgetting what is behind and straining toward what is ahead, I press on toward the goal to win the prize for which God has called me heavenward in Christ Jesus.

PHILIPPIANS 3:13-14

*W*hen there are disputes between husband and wife, their parents tend to take the side of their own children. Not Jean.

"I hate to have to admit it, but my son acted like a jerk," Jean says. "Gary and Beth's marriage was doomed early on, and to a large part it was his fault. But three wonderful things came out of their marriage: their daughter Suzanne, their son Robbie, and my daughter-in-law."

Throughout Gary and Beth's tumultuous ten years together, Jean took great pains to be supportive and encouraging. After their divorce, Jean asked Beth and the children to join her for dinner a couple of nights a week. She was faithful in including them on holidays, and she celebrated their birthdays with them.

"I never blamed Beth for the divorce," Jean says. "Everyone makes mistakes. Sure, there are things I would do differently than she does, but that doesn't make her way wrong. She knows I care about her and the children, and she always makes sure I am included in my grandchildren's doings—their school functions, soccer games, recitals, church activities—everything."

It's not that Jean has rejected her son. She sees him, too, and plays a part in his life with his new wife. But when he complained about her maintaining a relationship with Beth, she told him, "You brought her into my life, and I have learned to love her. You and she got a divorce, but I didn't divorce her. I welcomed her as my daughter-in-law, and I continue to love her. You'll just have to deal with it."

I won't say what I would do if I were in Jean's place. I don't know. But I do know Beth, and here's what she says: "Not a day goes by that I don't thank God for that wonderful woman. My children have a loving grandmother, and I have a wise and caring companion. She will never know the special place she has in our hearts."

"What I am doing," Jean says, "is remaining a link in that family chain. What could be more appropriate?"

***

Prayer for Today:
Father God, grant me the grace to put aside what is behind, and to press on toward what is today and what will be tomorrow.

The Parachute Dress

"You are the Christ, the Son of the living God."

MATTHEW 16:16

When I was eight years old, my mother made me a dress out of an old parachute my uncle brought home from the navy. My mother dyed the filmy nylon a beautiful shade of daffodil yellow and trimmed it with sunshine bright ribbon. When I wore that dress, I felt like a princess. I also felt invincible. I was, after all, wearing a parachute.

The first time I wore my new dress to Sunday school, I pranced around our upstairs Sunday school room, bragging to my friend Carol Ann. "I could jump out this window, and nothing would happen to me," I proclaimed as I pointed to the second-story window that overlooked the church entrance, "because my dress is a parachute!"

Carol Ann laughed. "I dare you to jump out that window!" she challenged.

Not for a moment did I doubt the power of my new dress. So I climbed onto the windowsill and prepared to demonstrate how gracefully I could float down to the sidewalk below. And just imagine the reception I'd get! Practically the entire congregation of our church was assembled down there.

But suddenly a horrifying thought occurred to me: If I were to jump out the window, everyone below me would be able to see my underwear! And for that reason alone, I climbed down and never tested the powers of my parachute dress.

Kids! To them, illusion is reality. If an idea makes sense to them, they are ready to act on it.

But as we mature, we learn to come to terms with reality. We learn that there are absolutes, both in our physical lives and in our spiritual lives. Perhaps the most basic, and most important, of these absolutes is a recognition of who Jesus Christ is and what relationship he has to God. Once we understand that, we have a firm foundation on which to build the rest of our lives.

Jesus is the Christ, the Son of the living God!

***

Prayer for Today:
Teach me, O Lord, to know you for who you are.

Tell Me a Story

"Lord, to whom shall we go? You have the words of eternal life."
JOHN 6:68

I should never ask Sage which story he wants me to tell him. His answer is always the same: "The alligator story!" He loves to hear me tell about casually meandering down to the river that runs behind a friend's home in Florida. He giggles with anticipation as I talk of sitting on the dock, dangling my feet in the water, watching the dragonflies skim past. His shoulders scrunch up and he shivers as I talk about watching the log floating in the distance. When I get to the two eyes in front of the log, he can stand it no longer.

"It's an alligator!" he yells. "Take your feet out of the water! It's an alligator!"

When I tell Sage the alligator story, he is right there on the dock with me. His feet are dangling in the water, too, and he sees that old alligator coming.

Stories have great power. They are word pictures that transport us to places we have never been, to times past and future. We can vicariously meet people we would never otherwise meet and experience things we would never experience. A good story lets us feel and hear and smell and taste. It lets us *see.*

The wonderful thing about a good story is that we cannot hear it too many times. Each time we listen, it takes us deeper into the experience and makes it more a part of us.

That's how it is with the story of Jesus—his birth, his life on earth, his horrible death, his resurrection and triumphant ascension. Throughout the past two thousand years, people have told and retold that story countless millions of times. Yet it grows sweeter with each telling.

That was certainly the opinion of Fanny Crosby, the blind saint who penned the words to the old hymn that ends with this refrain:

Tell me the story of Jesus,
Write on my heart every word.
Tell me the story most precious,
Sweetest that ever was heard.

***

Prayer for Today:
Open my eyes as I read the story of Jesus. Through it, teach me the stories of grace and love and forgiveness.

What Would You Change?

I consider that our present sufferings are not worth comparing with the glory that will be revealed in us.

ROMANS 8:18

A University of North Carolina research project asked four thousand retired executives what about their lives they'd change if they had it to do over again. The majority said they would rethink how they used their time. They wished they'd realized earlier that time is a nonrenewable asset and that they had made better use of the time they were given.

Each of us is accorded a space of time on this earth. For some of us, that span of time is longer than we ever expected. For others, it is much shorter. The length is not nearly as important as what we do with the time we are given.

When I was a child, our church newsletter had this motto: "Never give up. Keep right on keeping on, for God is still on the throne."

When I think of keeping on, I think of Tanzanian Olympic runner John Stephen Akhwari.

Late in the evening on October 20, 1968, after the sun had set and most of the spectators had left the Mexico City Olympic Stadium, the last of the marathon runners struggled across the finish line.

Suddenly the wail of police car sirens rang out, and all eyes were riveted on the gate. There a lone runner staggered into the stadium. John Akhwari was the last contestant to finish the grueling 26-mile 385-yard race. Early in the day his leg had been badly hurt in a fall, and crude bandages still clung to the injury. Slowly and painfully Akhwari managed to hobble the final lap around the track. As he approached the finish line, the spectators rose to applaud and cheer, just as though he were the winner.

After John Akhwari stumbled across the finish, a reporter asked him, "Why didn't you just quit?"

Akhwari replied, "My country did not send me seven thousand miles to start the race. They sent me to finish it."

When I come to the end of my life, I want the Father Almighty to greet me at heaven's gate with: "Well done, my good and faithful servant!"

～⚬～

Prayer for Today:

Help me, dear God, to spend whatever days you allow me faithfully running the race you set before me.

Real Grandmas

"Unless you change and become like little children, you will never enter the kingdom of heaven."

MATTHEW 18:3

*T*he term *grandmother* simply means the mother of someone who has children. She may or may not qualify as a *Real Grandma*. You know you are on the road to Real Grandmahood if you:

- Know to look for your kitchen utensils out in the sandbox.
- Have a sticky floor, a dirty oven, and happy grandkids.
- Know your grandchildren's favorite flavors of ice cream.
- Have at least one story the grandkids beg to hear again.
- Have lots of vases for surprise, freshly picked bouquets.
- Grow plenty of colorful flowers that can be picked for those bouquets.
- Have good stories about your grandchildren's parents' childhood that will make the kids snicker and the parents groan, "Oh, please, not that one!"
- Are willing to play board games (especially if the kids win).
- Never have to be asked by the kids if you love them because they can tell, but they ask anyway just to hear you say it.

I remember a little boy and his father in our neighborhood who wore matching T-shirts that said, "Any man can be a father, but it takes someone special to be a daddy." There's a lot to that. And it fits well with Grandmas, too.

Do you want to be a Real Grandma? Then ruffle up your hair and put on clothes that can be wrinkled and mussed. Put popcorn in the microwave (or a skillet, if you want to show the kids how it was done in the "olden days"). Arm yourself with a fun game, a couple of books, and maybe a pile of Play-Doh. Now call the grandkids to come over, then sit down. (That last part is really important because Real Grandmas always have laps.)

⚜

Prayer for Today:
May the words of my mouth and the meditations of my heart be acceptable in your sight, O Lord, my strength and my redeemer.

You Can Do Anything!

Deborah, a prophetess, the wife of Lappidoth, was leading Israel at that time. She held court under the Palm of Deborah ... and the Israelites came to her to have their disputes decided.

JUDGES 4:4-5

Consider:

- If Barbie were a real woman, she'd have to walk on all fours due to her "unique" proportions. (Besides which, her feet would be next to useless since she is permanently on her toes.)
- A psychological study in 1995 found that three minutes spent looking at models in a fashion magazine caused 70 percent of women to feel depressed, guilty, and shameful.
- If we are to believe the media, a woman who cares about herself should stay young forever—wrinkle-free, no gray hair, smooth hands, and of course, always slender and shapely.

Now consider this:

- The Civil Rights Movement was triggered by Rosa Parks, who was tired from working all day and could see no earthly reason to get up and give her seat on the bus to a man just because she was black and he was white, so she courageously said "No" and stayed in her seat.

- Beauty queen Esther put her life on the line by agreeing to use her tenuous position in the palace to implore the king to spare her people who, captives in a hostile land, were being threatened with extinction.
- Deborah led the Israelite army in battle because the commander of the army was scared.

As women, we can choose our role models. Some of us grew up warned that "women don't do that," or even worse, "women *can't* do that." Too many of us believed the warnings. But it's never too late to raise your sights.

To whom will you look as your role models?

~~~

Prayer for Today:

Help me to always keep my eyes looking up to the source of my true strength.

It's About Time

Jesus Christ is the same yesterday and today and forever.
HEBREWS 13:8

*M*y grandmother had a class picture of herself when she was seven years old. I looked and looked at that picture, and for the life of me I could never see my gray-haired grandma in that perky little girl with the long blond curls and the black button shoes.

I wonder what my grandchildren think when they see pictures of me as a child? I suppose they are as incredulous as I was.

Just imagine, as I write this, students entering college were born in 1981. So for them:

- There has always been a woman on the Supreme Court.
- They have never known a world without computers, Microsoft, fax machines, microwave ovens, in-line skates, or movies on videotape.
- The term *adult* has always been a synonym for "dirty."
- They were never concerned about the year 1984.
- They have no idea how big a breadbox is or how dumb a doornail might be.
- The war in Vietnam is as much ancient history as the Depression was to most of us.
- The Soviet Union ceased to exist before they were old enough to know what it was. "Cold War" is just a term from history—or more likely, a battle waged against a virus.

The world changes so quickly that we cannot take a nap without waking up old-fashioned. We've always exclaimed, "Where does the time go?" but now we hear that question coming from our children. We even hear our grandchildren asking it!

"Time waits for no man," the saying goes. Maybe not, but that doesn't take eternity into account. To get an idea of eternity, God gave us a glimpse of himself—unchanging, and unbound by time.

Prayer for Today:

Thank you for the comfort and security that come with knowing that you are the same today as you have always been, and that you will remain unchanged for the endless millennia to come.

The Golden Rule

"Do to others as you would have them do to you."

LUKE 6:31

One afternoon, Shaya, who is learning disabled, and his father came upon a group of boys playing baseball. As the two watched, Shaya asked, "Do you think you could get me into the game?"

Well aware that most kids would not want Shaya on their team, his father approached one of the boys and asked, "Do you think my son could get into the game?"

"Well," the boy said hesitantly, "we're losing by six runs and the game is in the eighth inning. I guess he can be on our team. We'll try to put him up to bat in the ninth inning."

Ecstatic, Shaya put on a glove and trotted out to center field. In the bottom of the eighth inning, Shaya's team scored a few runs but was still behind by three. In the bottom of the ninth, they scored again. Now, with two outs and the bases loaded and the potential winning runs on base, Shaya was scheduled to be up. To his father's amazement, Shaya was handed a bat. As he stepped awkwardly to the plate, the pitcher moved in a few steps and lobbed the ball softly. Shaya swung clumsily and missed.

A boy on Shaya's team came up and held the bat with him. The pitcher took a few more steps forward and tossed the ball gently. With his teammate's help, Shaya swung the bat, and together they hit a slow ground ball to the pitcher. The pitcher could easily have thrown the ball to the first baseman, and Shaya would have been out and the game over. Instead, he took the ball and threw it off to right field, beyond the first baseman's reach. Everyone started yelling, "Shaya, run to first!"

Never in his life had Shaya run to first, yet he scampered down the baseline. By the time he reached first base, the right fielder had the ball. Instead of throwing it to the second baseman, he threw it high over the third baseman's head.

"Run to second!" everyone cried.

Shaya ran toward second base as the runners ahead of him deliriously circled the bases toward home. As Shaya rounded third, the boys from both teams ran behind him screaming, "Shaya, run home!"

Shaya did, and all eighteen boys praised him for hitting the "grand slam" that won the game.

When we least expect it, and when we need it most, God's perfection shines through in the actions of his children.

***

Prayer for Today:
Help me, Lord, to show your perfection in the way I live.

Then Came Sunday

Praise be to the God and Father of our Lord Jesus Christ! In his great mercy he has given us new birth into a living hope through the resurrection of Jesus Christ from the dead, and into an inheritance that can never perish, spoil or fade—kept in heaven for you, who through faith are shielded by God's power until the coming of the salvation that is ready to be revealed in the last time.

1 PETER 1:3-5

It was Easter Sunday morning, and I had been anguishing all week about what kind of lesson to present to my third-grade Sunday school class. They had heard the story of Easter morning again and again. How could I make it come alive to them?

As I looked over the group of kids all dressed up in their Easter finery, I saw an unfamiliar face in the circle. "This is Atlas," Robert said. "He came with me today."

I greeted Atlas, then began: "Today we are going to talk about the death of Jesus...."

That's as far as I got. Atlas gasped, then exclaimed, "Jesus is dead? Jesus Rodriguez? He sits next to me in school!"

I explained that I was talking about Jesus Christ, God's Son.

"I don't know him," Atlas said.

"Well," I said to the other children, "we had better start at the beginning and tell the whole story. Who would like to start?"

Amy told about Jesus' birth and the angels and the shepherds and the star over Bethlehem. "That's why we celebrate Christmas," she explained.

John picked up the story and told about Jesus' miracles—healing the sick, making the blind to see, even raising the dead. Atlas' eyes grew round with wonder.

"If I'd been there, I would have made him king!" Atlas exclaimed.

"The people wanted to," Katy said. Then she told about the Palm Sunday procession with children waving palm branches and everyone shouting, "Hosannah!" Kevin interrupted to tell about Judas' betrayal, the trial, and finally the horrible crucifixion.

With tears streaming down his face, Atlas exclaimed, "Why did you have to tell me that story? I hate sad endings!"

"Oh, that's not the end!" Curtis said. And in a wonderfully impassioned way, he told the story of Easter morning.

When Curtis finished, for a few moments we all sat in silence. Then Atlas jumped to his feet and said, "I've got to get home and tell my mother about this! She'll like the way it ends!"

So do I, Atlas. So do I.

***

Prayer for Today:
Thank you, dear God, that you did not leave us with a sad ending. Thank you that there was Easter morning.

Relish the Moment

This is the day the Lord has made; let us rejoice and be glad in it.
PSALM 118:24

I took Josiah and Moses on a walk the other day. The day was warm and sunny, and the smell of ocean and jasmine wafted on the breeze. Behind us, the mountains spread out in all their majestic splendor. It was a gorgeous day for a walk.

But the two-year-old twins didn't breathe in the fragrance or admire the scenery. They were too busy looking at the details. One saw a bug crawling along the sidewalk. He crouched down and watched and watched until it ambled onto the grass and out of sight. The other spied a sprinkler head in the ground cover. He was totally engrossed with the mystery of the glistening silver object sparkling with drops of water. Other huge attention-getters were a worm in the gutter, a line of ants marching in formation, a discarded candy wrapper, a snail-munched dandelion, and a tarnished penny.

At each attraction, the boys would stop, get down close to look, watch, watch, then make joyful exclamations in two-year-old-"ese."

It was great fun to watch them, but I'll have to admit that at times I wanted to hurry them along. "We will never get to the end of the block if we don't keep moving," I said. And "Come on, now, that's just another bug. Let's keep going."

But the boys paid me no mind. They continued to stop and

look at every little thing.

Walking with Josiah and Moses taught me a wonderful lesson about life. Sooner or later we must realize that there is no destination, no final place of arrival. The true joy of life comes from taking the time to enjoy the walk.

Pause to look at the bugs and the sprinkler heads along your way today. Relish the moment and take time to enjoy the walk.

Prayer for Today:

Thank you, Father, for this day that you have made. May I take the time to rejoice and be glad in it.

Love Letters

What, then, shall we say in response to this? If God is for us, who can be against us?

ROMANS 8:31

*M*y friend Connie got a love note from her grand-baby-to-be. It was printed on a yellow note card trimmed with cuddly baby animals. It said:

Dear Grandma:

I'm not even born yet, and already you have been so good to me. Mommy and Daddy are really pleased that you love me so very much. Thank you for offering to take care of me when they are at work. I know we will be great friends, and that whatever happens, you will always be on my side.

I love you already!

Baby Jessica or Charles

P.S. I wanted to give you something special, and this was the most special thing I could think of.

Attached was a little box that contained a pacifier on a yellow ribbon.

What do you consider the most special and valuable love letter you've ever received? Did you say "the Bible"? If so, you are absolutely right. Every time you open God's Word, right there is his written message: *I love you so much that I sent my Son so that through him you can live forever.*

"Who shall separate us from the love of Christ?" the Apostle Paul asks in his letter to the Christians in Rome. "Shall trouble or hardship or persecution or famine or nakedness or danger or sword?" He answers his own question: "No, in all these things we are more than conquerors through him who loved us. For I am convinced that neither death nor life, neither angels nor demons, neither the present nor the future, nor any power, neither height nor depth, nor anything else in all creation, will be able to separate us from the love of God that is in Christ Jesus our Lord."

Now, that's what I call a love letter!

Prayer for Today:
Dear God, thank you for the love letter. May I keep it close beside me so that I can read it over and over and over again.

Light to My Eyes

The eye is the lamp of the body. If your eyes are good, your whole body will be full of light.

MATTHEW 6:22

Who was the most important person of the past millennium? In 1999, every publication and news program, it seemed, had its lists and its top choices. One man who made almost every list, and topped several, was Johannes Gutenberg, a well-born fifteenth-century German. He trained as a gem cutter, but soon became a partner in a printing shop in Strasbourg.

At that time, printing was a slow and laborious business. Each page printed required an entirely new printing form—usually a carved block of wood. Johannes Gutenberg was convinced that there had to be a better way. What if metal casts were to be made of the individual letters of the alphabet? That way a printer could use and reuse them in any order. Just about anything could be printed then. And a printer could make many copies of the same thing. Just imagine—printed books with a great number of pages!

In 1455, an amazing thing was unveiled at the Frankfurt Trade Fair. It was sections of the Latin Bible—printed! What a revelation: multiple copies of an entire volume produced by mechanical means!

By putting the Word of God directly into the hands of lay readers, movable type changed the world. No longer were people dependent upon what other people told them that the Bible said. Now they could read it for themselves. The new insights they gained helped to fuel the Protestant Reformation.

Of course, in the fifteenth century, few people could actually read. But there was another leap forward; now they had a reason to learn. There was a whole new emphasis put on literacy.

Today we take free access to God's Word for granted. I can't even tell you how many Bibles, in how many versions, we have in our house.

When I get to heaven, I'm going to say, "Thank you, Mr. Gutenberg. You truly were among the most important people of the first millennium A.D."

Prayer for Today:
Thank you for giving me the Word of God to be a lamp for my feet and a light for my path.

Blessed Pruning

Not only so, but we also rejoice in our sufferings, because we know that suffering produces perseverance; perseverance, character; and character, hope.

ROMANS 5:3-4

*D*an's son Toby has been working in our yard, and it has never looked so lush and fruitful. Seeing him at work on the fruit trees reminds me of when I first moved to this house, with my first husband. Back then we had just two trees, an orange and a peach. Unpruned, that peach tree grew big and full and leafy. It was loaded with peaches, although the fruit was disappointingly small and tasteless.

Then came the year my husband Larry was out of work. For the first time, he took his pruning shears to the peach tree. When I came home from school one day and saw how far back he had cut it, I stared in shock.

"You've killed it," I cried. "Now we won't have any peaches at all."

But I was wrong. That spring the pruned branches burst forth with a beautiful blanketing of pink blossoms. Soon little green peaches replaced the blossoms. "Leave them alone," I begged. Larry ignored me and thinned the fruit.

By the end of summer the branches were so heavily laden they had to be propped up. And the peaches—how large and sweet and juicy they were. There was no denying it: the tree was far better off for the painful trimming it had endured.

No one wants to be pruned. We don't like going through troubles and suffering and pain. I certainly don't. Not back then, and not in the years that followed. I didn't appreciate that period of joblessness. I railed against the fire that destroyed everything we owned. I hated it when Larry was diagnosed with an incurable disease.

But now, as I look back, I can see some wonderful fruit came about because of all that pruning. I learned lessons I never could have learned any other way.

When Phoenix saw Toby outside, pruning the trees, the other day, she asked me, "Doesn't it hurt them?"

"Maybe," I said. "But just wait until you see the fruit we'll have because of it!"

<hr />

Prayer for Today:
Help me, Lord, to patiently endure the cuts of the pruning shears. Let it make me fruitful rather than bitter.

Thank You, Lord

*Be joyful always; pray continually; give thanks in all circum-
stances, for this is God's will for you in Christ Jesus.*

1 THESSALONIANS 5:16-18

*H*ave you visited a nursing home lately? You might be
surprised at what you'll find. Certainly the people
there suffer from serious disabilities; that's why they're living in
a nursing home.

You'll probably see the usual activities: music, current events,
exercises, bingo. But you may well also see a smattering of
something new and unexpected. You may catch a glimpse of
"cyberseniors." Nursing home residents, it seems—even the
frail ones—are taking to computers surprisingly quickly.

Karla says, "My ninety-two-year-old grandmother Anna just
sent my daughter an e-mail at college! Can you imagine that?"

Anna's great-granddaughter e-mailed her back: "All my
friends agree that you are the coolest grandma!"

A determinedly independent person, Anna had not been at
all happy about having to give up her home and move into the
nursing home. For the first few months, she was downright
angry. "She disliked everything and everyone," Karla recalls.
"She wouldn't take part in the activities, she wouldn't
cooperate with efforts to get her involved with other residents,
she wouldn't even talk to her roommate."

One thing Anna did agree to do was attend the church
service held at the nursing home each Sunday afternoon. Four

local ministers took turns speaking at the service. Some she liked better than others, but she always attended. One Sunday the minister told the group, "Give thanks in all circumstances, for that is God's will."

Anna challenged him right then and there. "Wait a minute, young man! You mean I'm supposed to be thankful that I have to live here in this place?"

"Not *that* you live here," the pastor said. "Give thanks *even* here."

Anna agreed to start each day giving thanks. The very next morning she was asked if she wouldn't like to start working on the computer, and she reluctantly agreed.

"So I'm the 'coolest grandma'?" Anna now says with a smile. "Well, it's only because I decided to give thanks even here."

___

Prayer for Today:

Even when I cannot give thanks for *my circumstances, help me to give thanks* in *my circumstances.*

Trust Me!

Those who know your name will trust in you, for you, Lord, have never forsaken those who seek you.

PSALM 9:10

*W*hat have you learned in life?

A group of children were asked this question. Here are the answers three of them gave:

"Never ask your three-year-old brother to hold a tomato."
"You can't trust dogs to watch your food for you."
"Don't believe your sister if she says felt markers make good lipstick."

We all learn lessons in life, don't we? And many of those lessons have to do with trust. We are asked to place our trust in all kinds of things—stop lights, banks, airplanes, power lines, the ingredients in prepackaged foods, medications, diet books—and in many different people—friends, politicians, doctors, pharmacists, jury members, journalists. It doesn't take us long to learn that few people, and even fewer things, are really and truly trustworthy.

We may not always like what we read in God's Word. We may or may not realize that the reason we don't like what find in the Bible is that we cannot understand, or don't want to accept, God's ways. But if we look honestly at the past, one thing will be sure—*we can trust the Lord God.* In the end, when all is said and done, it will be perfectly clear that he is and always was infinitely trustworthy. We will see that never, ever—throughout all of history—did God forsake those who truly put their trust in him.

That's the lesson I have learned in life.

I, do, however, also have to agree with the stated lesson of one other child in the survey. That child said the lesson she had learned was: "The best place to be when you're sad is in grandma's lap."

Prayer for Today:
In you, O Lord, will I put my trust, for there is no other.

A Long Life

I long to dwell in your tent forever and take refuge in the shelter of your wings.

PSALM 61:4

Remember Ponce de León and his desperate search for the Fountain of Youth? His quest has been the quest of men and women down through the ages. And it is still our quest today. If we can't have eternal youth, then at least we want a long, long life.

Hezekiah was one of the good kings of Israel. Unlike his wicked father—who went so far as to sacrifice one of his own sons to the idol Baal!—Hezekiah tore down the idols and led the people back to God. And looking to God, he fought successfully against the marauding Assyrians.

But while he was still a middle-aged man (for those days, at least—he was probably only about thirty-seven!) Hezekiah took sick. He was so ill that the prophet Isaiah came to him and warned, "The Lord says you are to put your house in order because you are not going to get well. You're going to die."

Die! After all the good he had done for his people? After all he had done for *God?* Hezekiah didn't like that prediction one bit. So he turned his face to the wall and cried, "Please, please, God, let me live! Remember all the good I have done and let me live!"

God answered Hezekiah's prayer.

But Hezekiah is a striking example of the truth that there is more to longevity than just staying alive. He lived for fifteen more years and in that time did so much harm to the country that instead of being remembered mainly as a good and godly king, he is remembered as the one who set Israel up for the horrible Babylonian captivity.

What would you be willing to do in order to extend your life? Certainly we are wise to watch what we eat, get exercise, wear seat belts when we ride in a car, and do the other good-sense things that help us stay well and healthy. But we are also wise to be fully aware that our days are properly numbered by God.

There is indeed more to longevity than just staying alive.

<center>~~~</center>

Prayer for Today:

Lord, rather than seeking for a longer life or endless youth, let my quest be for a double portion of your Spirit.

Only Child

"The Lord bless you and keep you; the Lord make his face shine upon you and be gracious to you; the Lord turn his face toward you and give you peace."

NUMBERS 6:24-26

It had been a hard day, and Phoenix spent the night with us. We made chocolate pudding, then we ate popcorn while we watched a video. When bedtime came, she and I snuggled down together and read books until it was past time to turn out the light.

The next morning I made hot oatmeal for breakfast—Phoenix's favorite. It was a chilly morning, so I wrapped a snuggly quilt around her for her ride to school.

When we got to school, instead of getting out of the car, Phoenix sat and sat. Finally she sighed and said, "I like being an only child."

I know exactly how she feels. There were six children in my family, and for part of my growing up years my parents had foster children as well. Opportunities to be snuggled in a blanket, to have special foods prepared just for me, to sleep in the big bed—even to sleep alone!—were few and far between.

Sure it's great to have other kids around, but sometimes...

Enter Grandma. We can let each of our grandchildren have a chance to be an only child. One at a time, we can give them a little individual pampering. We can make their favorite foods just for them. We can read their favorite books. We can play games with them and let them win. They don't have to share, they don't have to be good sports, and they don't have to set an example for anyone.

In this way, we can pronounce a blessing on each one of our precious grandchildren. Our grandchildren may not actually be "onlies," yet every single one of them is a precious one of a kind.

─────

Prayer for Today:
Bless each of my grandchildren, O Lord. Be gracious to every one. Make your face to shine upon each one, and give each child your peace.

Older Than Who?

*Surely goodness and love will follow me all the days of my life, and
I will dwell in the house of the Lord forever.*

PSALM 23:6

There was a big dispute among the members of the Bible
study that meets at my house. One woman had had the
audacity to refer to us as "the older women of the church" and
others were up in arms about it. One woman suggested we call
ourselves M&Ms (mature and magnificent). Another preferred
WOW (women of wisdom).

After we broke up for the evening, I sat for a good while and
pondered: How come we think of old things so differently than
we think of old people? Old china, old trees, old furniture, old
pictures—we appreciate these things precisely for their oldness.
Their beauty increases with their years and with the memories
they hold. Even if they are not useful or beautiful, we still see
them as valuable.

How come we don't give the same appreciation to old
people? Sure, older folks have oddities and eccentricities, but
isn't that what gives them character? Those differences could be
looked upon as a source of strength. They might actually
become the most interesting parts of who those people are.

In Genesis 5:27 we read: "Altogether, Methuselah lived 969
years, and then he died." 969 years? Wow! What a lot of character he must have had!

Let us grandmothers vow to celebrate the oldness we see

around us. Let us determine to look into an older face and see something beautiful, important, and valuable there. Let us remind ourselves, as well as those around us, how much richer we are because of the aged among us. Let us love and respect the wisdom, experience, passion, and power they carry within them.

Then let us ask ourselves: "How will I age? Who and what will I be when I am old?" Perhaps the answer will be M&M or WOW.

Prayer for Today:
Dear Lord, grant that goodness and love will follow me all the days of my life, and let me dwell with you forever.

"Real" Theology

And this is my prayer: that your love may abound more and more in knowledge and depth of insight, so that you may be able to discern what is best and may be pure and blameless until the day of Christ.

PHILIPPIANS 1:9-10

*N*ot all children's books are just children's books. Take for instance *The Velveteen Rabbit* by Margery Williams. There is some pretty good theology in there.

The Velveteen Rabbit is a toy bunny who sees a group of real rabbits that, unlike himself, can stretch and hop. From that day on he has one desperate desire—to be a real rabbit. It's all he can think about, even though he's not sure what "real" actually means.

One morning in the nursery, the Velveteen Rabbit asks the wise old skin horse, "What is Real? Does it mean having things that buzz inside you and a stick-out handle?"

"Real isn't how you are made," the skin horse tells him. "It's a thing that happens to you." Later he explains, "Generally, by the time you are Real, most of your hair has been loved off, and your eyes drop out and you get loose in the joints and very shabby. But these things don't matter at all, because when you are Real you can't be ugly, except to people who don't understand."

There is wisdom for us grandmas in the skin horse's words. As we grow older, more experienced in life, and more secure in ourselves, it should become easier for us to be real. The pressure—both from inside and from out—to always look good is not as strong. It's great to be able to be seen and appreciated as we really are—even if our hair is getting loved off, our eyes are dropping out, or our joints are loose. Yes, even if our bodies have grown very, very shabby.

How great it is to be able to appreciate ourselves not in *spite* of the years we have lived and the roads we have traveled, but *because* of them.

Isn't it great to be real?

━━━

Prayer for Today:
Help me to be real in my desire for godly wisdom and in my love for those things that are excellent and sincere.

Life Wisdom

I will instruct you and teach you in the way you should go; I will counsel you and watch over you.

PSALM 32:8

*J*t was just weeks before my family and I were to leave for our trip to England, and my list of things to do was pages long. An eighty-five-year-old attorney friend of ours called and advised, "Before you take a trip like that you should get your house appraised and make sure your homeowners insurance is adequate."

"Good idea," I told him. "I'll put it on my to-do list."

I did—on the bottom.

Several days later he called again. "Did you check your insurance?" he asked.

"No," I said, "but I will just as soon as I get to it."

More days passed and he called again. "Have you done it yet?" he asked.

"No," I told him, "but I will."

By now the calls were daily. He was annoyingly persistent. Finally, just to get him off my back, I said, "All right! I'll do it today." We had our house appraised and discovered that it was way underinsured, so we increased our fire insurance.

Three weeks later, while we were in England, our house burned to the ground. We had made one three-dollar payment for the new policy that doubled our insurance.

Later I asked our friend, "What ever made you insist that we check our insurance?"

"It was just good advice," he said. "I've learned from experience."

Simply by living life and experiencing its ups and downs, we do gain insights and wisdom. We learn to see things that younger people with less experience miss. That's good. What isn't so good is when people expect us to have wisdom in all things simply because we are older than they are.

Believing you have to be wise is a terrible burden. It's awful to feel obligated to dispense wisdom on the spur of the moment. Perhaps it will help to remember this: You will inspire your grandchildren through the way you live your life much more than through the wise things you say.

Prayer for Today:
Help me to live the wisdom I have gained in life, and only to speak when I really have something to say.

Change for the Better

For we are God's workmanship, created in Christ Jesus to do good works, which God prepared in advance for us to do.

EPHESIANS 2:10

As my grandfather grew older, his unique traits became idiosyncrasies. By the time he was in his nineties, they had become obsessions. First he was thrifty. Then his thrift turned to stinginess. In his last years he took to hiding money in the lining of his coat and sleeping with his wallet under his mattress.

It does seem that whatever a person's traits, as he or she gets older, those characteristics are accentuated. Doesn't it make sense, then, to use that natural progression for good? Wouldn't it be great if, before we are too old, we could build up the positive side of our characteristics and diminish the negative? That way the traits accentuated would be the positive traits. For instance:

- Instead of growing more stubborn we can become more steadfast and dependable.
- Instead of becoming more complacent we can become more peaceful.
- Instead of more financially irresponsible we can become more generous.
- Instead of obsessive we can grow more focused.
- Instead of growing irritable we can become alert to the

areas of life where we can facilitate changes for the better.

Life experience deepens our understanding of ourselves. With time, we become more able to identify those aspects of ourselves we aren't pleased with—if we are willing to see them, that is.

Do you ever lie in bed at night unable to sleep? Those irritating nighttime hours can be a wonderful opportunity to contemplate and pray. Try it. Pray that God will guide you as you choose which elements of your personality to develop and which to squelch. Ask him to take the changes and restrictions of your future and to use them as opportunities. Ask him to make you more understanding, more compassionate, and more patient, slower to speak and quicker to listen.

Changes can tear down or they can build. The choice is yours.

━━◆◆◆◆━━

Prayer for Today:
Thank you, Lord, for the changes that will come my way. Please use them to make me more like you.

Dead or Alive

"Whoever welcomes a little child like this in my name welcomes me."
MATTHEW 18:5

*M*y first two books were written for children. A couple of years after *John Newton: The Angry Sailor* came out I received a letter from a little girl in Oklahoma named Nicole. On lined pink paper decorated with black and white bunnies, she had printed in block letters:

Deer Mrs. Strom,

I liked the book you wrote. You write good and interesting. I really liked it when John Newton got stuck on that island and when his boat got smashed apart and he had to tie it together with ropes and stuff.
I like you too. Would you write to me?

Love, Nicole
P.S. Are you dead or alive? If you're dead you don't have to answer this letter.

How could I not answer that letter—especially since I was alive?

Remember when you were a child, how interesting old people were (and anyone over thirty-five was old!)? Remember how you liked to hear about ancestors, maybe even ancestors in the faith like John Newton?

For many people, that interest and curiosity get crowded out in the early teen years, then continue to get shoved into the background during the busy, active years that follow. For the fortunate among us, curiosity resurfaces as our lives begin to slow down a bit.

As grandmothers, it's shocking to realize that we now *are* ancestors! No wonder so many of us find ourselves becoming more interested in family history. The great thing is that as we reach backward and extend our lives behind us, we are also reaching forward and extending it to the generations to come.

As for me, I am interested and curious. And I am alive, so I will answer!

Prayer for Today:

Keep me mindful that my actions today will reach down to my children and grandchildren, and on to the generations to follow. Help me to live worthily.

Count the Cost

All a man's ways seem right to him, but the Lord weighs the heart.
PROVERBS 21:2

Carolyn and her daughter Jana are hardly speaking. The sticking point? Grandma Carolyn's involvement in granddaughter Shelby's upbringing.

"I want my mother to be less involved in the way I'm raising my child," Jana says with more than a touch of bitterness. "Sure I'm a single mom. Sure I'm struggling to get by. Sure I made my share of mistakes. But Shelby is my daughter, and I have the right to raise her as I see fit."

Carolyn sees it differently. "Jana works part time and barely earns enough to cover her and Shelby's basic needs. For anything extra, she looks to me. I don't even care to count the number of times I have bailed her out when she couldn't pay her rent."

"The reason I can't always make the rent is because my mother insists that Shelby needs to be raised in a certain neighborhood, and rent is considerably higher here," Jana counters. "And why do I work part time? Because Mother insists that I spend time home with Shelby."

"And what's wrong with that?" Carolyn bristles. "So I want my grandchild living in a safe and attractive area where she can go to good schools. So I understand the importance of being home with children when they are little. Goodness knows I sacrificed to be there for my own children. Does wanting the best for Shelby make me a bad grandmother?"

Carolyn and Jana are not unusual. In these days of high costs, even two-parent families often turn to their own parents for financial help. But it is almost a given that financial help comes with strings attached.

"I appreciate her help," Jana says, "I really do. But I don't want her opinions."

Says Carolyn, "I'm a mother and a grandmother. When I see things that need to be said, I have a responsibility to say them."

Dependence and independence each has its cost. Count that cost, then decide, *Is it worth it?*

<hr>

Prayer for Today:
My ways do seem right to me, dear Lord. So, please, weigh my heart. Show me where to hold tight and where to loosen my grip.

Signs and Labels

But the fruit of the Spirit is love, joy, peace, patience, kindness, goodness, faithfulness, gentleness and self-control. Against such things there is no law.

GALATIANS 5:22-23

I taught school at an air force base during the Vietnam War. Because pilots constantly flew between our base and Indochina, everyone on the base had to have regular inoculations for plague. That was no minor shot, believe me. It hurt! And it kept on hurting. The arm that got the injection was exquisitely painful for a couple of days. So I laminated a sign that said "PLAGUE SHOT" and hung it around the neck of whoever had just been inoculated—including myself. And because everyone knew how it felt, everyone treated the afflicted person with tenderness and care.

Unfortunately, many labels aren't that helpful. They affect the labeled person in various ways.

Some categorize a person:

"She's the musical one."

"He's the computer whiz."

Some restrict a person:

"She's a slow learner."

"He's sickly."

Some are demeaning and hurtful:

"She's fat and lazy."

"He's the grumpy one of the family."

Of course, there are also those that encourage:

"She's always so loving and kind."

"You hardly ever see him without a smile on his face."

Attaching labels to a person can be serious business. Many children are pegged forever by the labels attached by the people closest to them.

But for Christians, the Holy Spirit attaches a special list of labels, and all of them are positive and encouraging: loving, joyful, peaceful, patient, kind, good, faithful, gentle, and self-controlled.

What a wonderful way to be labeled through life.

***

Prayer for Today:
Dear God, please attach to me the first and foremost label of all: Christian, which means "little Christ." And help me to live worthy of the name.

What's This World Coming To?

To us a child is born, to us a son is given, and the government will be on his shoulders.

ISAIAH 9:6

*F*or my fiftieth birthday, I received a most interesting gift: A copy of the newspaper, the *San Francisco Call Bulletin*, for the day I was born (I was born in San Francisco). There are articles about the atrocities during the Holocaust in Europe and crime in San Francisco. The headline reads: *Harlem Riots Kill 6*.

I can just see people reading the paper that morning. They probably shook their heads, clucked their tongues, and exclaimed, "What *is* this world coming to?"

I remember hearing my grandparents say that. I remember hearing my parents say it. And yes, I have said it myself.

I don't suppose there has ever been an age that didn't abound with warnings and dire pronouncements about the decline of the times.

When the Israelites were carried off to captivity in Babylon, they wept bitterly the entire way. Their country was gone! What was the world coming to?

It took seventy years, but things got better. The Jews did go home again.

My grandfather told me about people who committed suicide during the Great Depression. "Times were so bad, they just couldn't believe things would ever be right again," he said.

Things did get better. In fact, many of the people who lived through the Depression also saw the greatest prosperity the country had ever known.

At the beginning of World War II, after it became obvious that the Allies' policy of appeasing Adolf Hitler had failed to stop his plans for conquest and war, one British leader described the dark situation in unforgettable terms. "The lamps are going out all over Europe," he said, "and we shall not see them lit again in our lifetime."

He was wrong. Just a few years later Europe did indeed see the lights lit again.

What is this world coming to?

To God. In his time. And when that happens, the government will be on his shoulders, and peace will reign forever and ever.

Prayer for Today:

Thank you, dear God, for what this world is coming to. Thank you that you alone are in charge of the future just as you were in charge of the past and are in charge of the present.

Shepherd Me, Lord

The Lord is my shepherd, I shall not be in want.

PSALM 23:1

I have always loved lambs. My stuffed lamb Snowflake is the first toy I remember, and I loved him for years. On my tenth birthday, I got a new stuffed lamb, Snowball, and I started a collection. It grew and grew, but when our house burned, all my lambs were destroyed. After the fire, I referred to those lambs in my speaking, and I wrote about them in my books and articles. An amazing thing happened. People all over the world started sending me lambs. All kinds of lambs—stuffed, ceramic, embroidered, big and small and every size in between. Plaid ones from Scotland, a spun wool one from Austria, a folded paper lamb from Japan.

My grandchildren love my lambs. There is a pile of stuffed lambs on my cedar chest in the bedroom, and when they come over they head right to the lamb pile. Last year for Christmas, my husband Dan got me a beautifully crafted shepherd who now stands among my sheep.

It has been suggested that of all the names for God, none is as comforting as *Shepherd*. I agree. In biblical times, shepherds cared for their sheep in so many ways. Sheep depended upon the shepherd for everything in their lives—even to put them back on their feet if they fell into a ditch. The shepherd knew every one of them by name, and the sheep knew the voice of their shepherd.

I have heard many negative references to us as sheep: frightened, passive, foolish, blind followers. I prefer to see us as obedient followers who walk after our shepherd in the right places and the right ways. As a shepherd cares for, feeds, and guards his sheep, our Great Shepherd cares for, feeds, and guards us.

And he knows us, and he calls us by name.

<hr>

Prayer for Today:
Thank you, dear God, for being my shepherd. Thank you for caring for me and loving me more than any earthly shepherd ever could.

Abba, Father

All good giving, every perfect gift, comes from above, from the Father.
JAMES 1:17, NEB

In Armenia in 1989, after a devastating earthquake, a father rushed to his son's school to find him. The school was gone. All that remained of it was a pile of rubble. The father hurried to the place where his son's classroom had been and started frantically digging with his bare hands.

"It's no use," other grief-stricken parents told him. "Our children are gone."

Officials, fearing fires and explosions, did their best to get the man to leave. But all alone, with his hands raw and bleeding, the father kept right on digging through the rubble.

After forty hours, the father uncovered his son and thirteen other children. They were still alive.

"I told the other kids not to worry," the boy told his father. "I told them that if you were still alive, you'd save me."

That boy put all his faith in his father, and his trust was well founded. His father had come through for him just as the boy knew he would.

How much more can we put our trust in our heavenly Father. He is, after all, the maker of the heavens and the earth. And he is filled with love, mercy, and compassion for his children. In fact, he is the very source of these attributes. We can turn to him in our times of distress. He understands our frailties, and he gently tends us even in our weakest hour.

The Apostle Paul writes that we can come boldly before God and that we can call him "Abba, Father." How it must have shocked the Christians in Rome when they got that letter! Walk right up to the Ruler of the Universe and call him "Daddy"?

That's right!

God is not only our dear Father, but he is our everlasting Father. He will be there for us forever and ever.

***

Prayer for Today:

My Father in heaven, hallowed be your name. Your kingdom come, your will be done on earth as it is in heaven. Give me today my daily bread. Forgive me my debts, as I also have forgiven my debtors. And lead me not into temptation, but deliver me from the evil one. For yours is the power and the glory for ever and ever. Amen.

Grandma Highs

The Lord loves righteousness and justice; the earth is full of his unfailing love.

PSALM 33:5

*W*e grandmothers are the grateful recipients of certain things that just naturally lift us to a higher plane. I realize each of us has our own things that give us a special "Grandma high." Let me share my list with you, then you can add all those things that round out your own personal list.

I get a Grandma high from:

- Seeing my grandchildren do something for the first time.
- Knowing I taught the little one that new thing.
- Hearing my grandchildren call out joyful greetings when they see me and come running to give me hugs.
- Watching the full moon with my grandchild and seeing a shooting star streak across the night sky.
- Walking together barefoot through soft, freshly cut grass.
- Walking together barefoot in the sand along the seashore.
- Sitting in front of a fire, sipping hot chocolate with candy canes.
- Smelling the fragrant roses that grow in front of the house.
- Watching the waves roll onto the beach—and now and then seeing a dolphin leap out in the ocean.
- Collecting things together, like seashells and pretty rocks and colorful autumn leaves.

- Blowing bubbles together and seeing the rainbows in them.
- Making Play-Doh snakes and having snake fights.
- Rowdying around together like we don't have the brains we were born with.
- Hearing a grandbaby say "Gamma."
- Watching the birds in the birdfeeder and chasing away the blue jay bully.
- Baking Christmas cookies together—or any other kind of cookies, for that matter.
- Getting gooey cookie-dough kisses from loving little lips.
- Reading stories with happy endings.

Don't you agree that Grandma highs more than make up for any of life's lows?

***

Prayer for Today:
Open my eyes, dear Lord, so that I can see your unfailing love everywhere around me, especially in the lives of my grandchildren.

For the Love of a Grandcat

But the plans of the Lord stand firm forever, the purposes of his heart through all generations.

PSALM 33:11

Before I had grandkids, I had grandcats. My daughter loved those cats, and I loved my daughter, so when she and her husband moved from Toronto, Canada, to southern California, I agreed to help out. I helped them pack then drove with them to Detroit, where I was to fly home with Pierre and Felix. I checked the animal carrier in, then I boarded the plane.

I was eager to be on my way, but the plane just sat there and sat there. Finally an airline attendant made her way back to me and said, "Mrs. Strom? Please get your things together and get off the plane."

"Why?" I asked.

"I don't know," she said. "But we can't take off until we have you off the plane."

Everyone stared as I walked down the aisle.

At the door of the plane stood two men with badges marked *Airport Security*. "Are you Mrs. Strom?" they asked.

I said I was and asked what in the world was going on.

"Your cats got loose," one said. "We need you to catch them."

So while my plane flew off into the wild blue yonder, I was escorted to a closed runway and was given a yellow vest and a guest security badge. "We caught one cat," I was told, "but the other one is under one of those vehicles out on the runway."

I spent the next two hours crawling around under vehicle after vehicle calling, "Here, Felix! Come on, kitty!" I was just about ready to give up when an orange paw reached down from somewhere up under a baggage truck.

Fifteen minutes later, with two terrified cats back in their carrier, I was escorted to the baggage counter. "The last flight is just leaving for Los Angeles," I was told. "If you run, you just might make it."

So I ran. As I got to the gate, I saw myself reflected in the window. What a sight! My hair was sticking up, my clothes were disheveled, and I had black grease on my face and down the front of me. But I made it onto the plane just as the door was being closed. I found my seat and gratefully sank down.

The man next to me looked me up and down, then he said, "Rough flight, huh?"

What a grandma won't do!

<hr>

Prayer for Today:
Thank you, Lord, that in the good times and the bad, your plans stand firm.

Heavenly Gifts

"If you, then, though you are evil, know how to give good gifts to your children, how much more will your Father in heaven give good gifts to those who ask him!"

MATTHEW 7:11

*D*an and I just got back from Hawaii, where we were speaking at a conference. It was stormy most of the time we were there. That was fine with us; we were worn out from hectic schedules and were looking forward to getting some rest. We didn't snorkel or hike, but of course we took time to shop.

When we got home, we couldn't wait to pull out the gifts we had brought for the grandkids. Of course they all got the obligatory T-shirts. For Sage we brought a surfer necklace (we told him it was like something his surfing uncle Toby might wear) and for Phoenix a necklace with a shark's tooth on it. We also brought shell necklaces for each of them and chocolate macadamia nuts for everyone.

Isn't it fun to get gifts for grandchildren? They don't have to be expensive or flashy presents. They don't even have to be toys or candy. But it's hard to be anywhere, it seems, and not see things you just know they will enjoy.

We are such imperfect people. Our motivations are tangled and in many ways self-serving. Yet we know how to give good gifts. We know to check for age appropriateness, to think about sugar content, to watch out for small pieces that might be dangerous to the little ones. If we can give good and loving gifts, just imagine what God can do!

Sometimes our grandchildren take our gifts for granted. Sometimes we wish they wouldn't greet us with, "Did you bring me anything?"

Imagine how God must feel (although comparing divine feelings with human feelings is probably foolish). Still, we certainly do tend to take his gifts to us for granted—especially we who live such blessed and prosperous lives in the West. And in our prayers we do tend to dwell on, "What are you going to give me? Here's what I want today."

From our grandchildren, we can learn lessons in gift giving and also in gift receiving.

***

Prayer for Today:
Dear God, I know that every good and every perfect gift comes from you. Please accept my grateful thanks.

The Green-Haired Kid

I thank my God every time I remember you.

reat! Just great! I thought with disgust as I saw who my seatmate would be on a flight from Los Angeles to Des Moines.

The young man who had just slumped down beside me was dressed in tattered jeans and a dingy T-shirt. His arms and fingers were decorated with tattoos. And his hair, which reached to the center of his back, was dyed bright green. I squeezed close to the window and buried myself in a manuscript I was proofreading.

Throughout the first half of the flight I listened as fellow passengers commented on the "guy with the green hair." My seatmate seemed not to hear, although I couldn't see how that was possible.

When dinner was served, the young man gobbled up everything on his tray. Since I wasn't going to eat my cake, I asked him if he would like it.

"Yeah, sure! Thanks a lot," he said. "I'm really hungry."

I smiled and nodded as I handed him my roll as well.

"Is that a manuscript you're reading?" he asked, his mouth filled with cake. "It looks interesting." Then he added, "I'd like to be a writer someday."

We started to chat. The green-haired kid told me about a really funny book he was reading and asked if I'd like to hear some of it. I said I would.

During the rest of the trip, we laughed and talked and laughed some more. We had a great time, the green-haired kid and I. I was even able to say something about the important place God holds in my life. He said he liked that.

When the plane landed, the green-haired kid said, "Thanks a lot for talking to me. No one ever does."

"It was my pleasure," I told him, and I really meant it.

I hope I encouraged that young man. He certainly encouraged me. I hope I built him up a little. He built me up a lot. I hope, somehow, I helped him toward the kingdom of God. He helped me appreciate a heavenly Father who looks beyond green hair and tattooed arms.

※

Prayer for Today:
Thank you, God, for bringing the green-haired kid into my life. Help me to grow more and more into a person who does not judge people by appearance.

A Forgiving Heart

Create in me a pure heart, O God, and renew a steadfast spirit within me.

PSALM 51:10

*J*n her book *The Hiding Place*, Corrie ten Boom tells the terrifying story of how her family hid Jews from the Nazis in Holland, then were themselves captured to suffer in the Ravensbruck death camp. Her sister Betsie died there. Two years after Corrie was released, she returned to the site of the camp, where she gave a message to a group of Germans who had come to hear her. Her theme was forgiveness.

After her talk, a man strode forward, thrust out his hand, smiled and said, "A fine message, Fräulein! How good it is to know that, as you say, all our sins are at the bottom of the sea!"

The man didn't recognize Corrie, but she recognized him immediately. He had been one of the cruelest guards at the camp. Corrie writes:

And I, who had spoken so glibly of forgiveness, fumbled in my pocketbook rather than take that hand. He would not remember me, of course—how could he remember one prisoner among those thousands of women?

But I remembered him and the leather crop swinging from his belt. I was face-to-face with one of my captors and my blood seemed to freeze.

"You mentioned Ravensbruck in your talk," he was saying. "I was a guard there." No, he did not remember me.

"But since that time," he went on, "I have become a Christian. I know that God has forgiven me for the cruel things I did there, but I would like to hear it from your lips as well. Fräulein,"—again the hand came out—"will you forgive me?"

And I stood there—I whose sins had again and again been forgiven—and could not forgive. Betsie had died in that place—could he erase her slow terrible death?

It could not have been many seconds that he stood there—hand held out—but to me it seemed hours as I wrestled with the most difficult thing I had ever had to do.

Through the grace of God, Corrie ten Boom was able to forgive that man.

But only through God's grace.

That is the only way any of us can forgive anyone.

Prayer for Today:

Only you can both forgive and forget, dear God. I cannot help but remember. But help me to be willing to forgive as you in your mercy have forgiven me.

Precious Things

Better a meal of vegetables where there is love than a fattened calf with hatred.

PROVERBS 15:17

Periodically Juanita has asked each of her grandchildren, "What would you especially like me to leave you when I am gone?"

When she asked this question of eleven-year-old Kristin, the girl's first response was concern. "Grammy, you aren't going to die, are you?" she asked anxiously.

"No, no," said Juanita. "Not for a long time. But I have made out my will, and I want to make sure that I set aside something for you that you really like."

Kristin mumbled something noncommittal and Grandma let it pass. Maybe Kristin was too young for such a question.

Later that day Kristin said, "I know what I want, Grammy. When you're gone, I want you to leave me the Mrs. Doubtfire mugs."

Juanita had a set of mugs she used to serve hot cocoa with marshmallows to her grandchildren. One rainy day she and Kristin were watching the movie *Mrs. Doubtfire*, and they saw the very same mugs. They stopped the video and rushed to the kitchen to get the cocoa mugs to compare. Sure enough, they were exactly the same. So they kept the video paused long enough to make nice steaming mugs of hot cocoa with marshmallows to drink while they finished the movie.

Juanita had many beautiful things—crystal, silver, jewelry, antiques, handmade quilts. But of all her possessions, the most precious to Kristin were the Mrs. Doubtfire mugs. Why? Because while those other things may have had more cash value, the cocoa mugs were the things that, for her, contained the essence of her grandmother.

We as a society are well schooled in recognizing, protecting, and insuring things with cash value. But what about the things that hold emotional value? Are we as careful with them?

Take some time to take stock of those things that are most valuable to you. How will you protect and honor them? How will you hold them close? How will you pass them on?

___

Prayer for Today:

Help me to see the value and beauty in the things that are truly valuable to me. Help me never to be blinded by the glittering things that only look valuable because society tells me they are.

Lessons Learned Well

Carry each other's burdens, and in this way you will fulfill the law of Christ.

GALATIANS 6:2

J was sitting in church behind a family with two young children. Behind Mama's back the little girl pinched her brother, who responded by letting out a loud wail. As Daddy was hurrying the boy out, his sister looked after him with a smirk, then she stuck out her tongue.

Their shenanigans made me smile. They were generally well-behaved children. The thing that bothered me most was what happened after the service. Mama said to the little girl, "You tell your brother you're sorry."

The girl pouted and hung her head.

"Say it!" Mama said with a threatening voice. "Look at him and say 'I'm sorry!'"

Grudgingly the girl mumbled a less than half-hearted "I'm sorry."

"Now tell your brother you love him."

The little girl stubbornly shook her head no.

"Say it!" Mama ordered. "If you don't, I'll have to spank you."

The little girl mumbled "I love you" but her voice and her face spoke of anything but love.

It made me think of something Mark Twain, the writer and humorist, once wrote. He was no man of God, but he did have a good deal of insight into the human condition. He said: "We should be careful to get out of an experience only the wisdom that is in it—and stop there; lest we be like the cat that sits down on a hot stove lid. She will never sit down on a hot stove lid again—and that is well; but also she will never sit down on a cold one any more."

It makes me wonder. What are the lessons our little ones are really learning when we force them to say such things as "I'm sorry" and "I love you"? Are we teaching them to truly ask forgiveness or encouraging them to really love? What about when we force them to "Kiss Great-Aunt Louise" or "Give the nice man a hug"? Could it be that we are just teaching them to lie or maybe even to submit to a dangerous situation?

Wouldn't it be wonderful if we could teach our little ones to empathize with the other person? Then we would be taking a great stride toward showing them what it means to carry each other's burdens.

Prayer for Today:
Help me, Lord, to understand the difference between lessons that force a child to speak and act in a certain way, and those that reach their hearts and affect who they are.

The Hidden Gift

I have no greater joy than to hear that my children are walking in the truth.

3 JOHN 4

I was getting ready to have a garage sale, and my mother contributed a couple of boxes of stuff. There were lamps and housewares and clothes, and there were some of my grand-father's things as well. My grandfather had died the year before, and my mother had just cleaned out his closet.

As I was putting everything out on display, my son Eric came out to help. He was thirteen and very cool. So it surprised me when he picked up one of Granddad's sport jackets and said, "Hey, this isn't bad." He put it on, turned up the collar and rolled up the sleeves, then asked, "What do you think?"

"It's great," I said. "If you want it, you can have it. Consider it a gift from your great-granddad."

Eric took the jacket to his room. A few minutes later he came back outside with a strange look on his face. "Look what I found," he said. He held out a handful of twenty-dollar bills.

Granddad, in his last years, had become so suspicious and paranoid that he had taken to hoarding money and hiding it in the lining of his jacket.

"It's for you," I told Eric. "It's a legacy from your great-grandfather. What are you going to do with it?"

Eric spent a good deal of time contemplating that question. He wanted to use it for something that would have pleased his great-grandfather.

Finally he made his decision. "I'm going to buy a camera," Eric told us.

Granddad would indeed have been pleased to see what Eric did with that camera. Eric was photographer for his high school yearbook and newspaper. Throughout his teens he earned extra money shooting special events; he was photographer for his aunt's wedding; he even flirted with the idea of becoming a photojournalist.

Granddad never knew about the camera he gave his great-grandson. Likely you'll never know about the legacy gifts you give your grandchildren and great-grandchildren either. Nor will I.

Oh, that my legacy could be that they walk in the truth!

Prayer for Today:
Thank you for the joy you give me in my grandchildren. Please, dear Lord, teach them to walk in your truth.

Lost Things

No eye has seen, no ear has heard, no mind has conceived what God has prepared for those who love him.

1 CORINTHIANS 2:9

We were in Oxford, England, when we received the news that a devastating fire was burning out of control in our hometown of Santa Barbara, California. Before the day was over, we learned that our home had burned to the ground. Everything we owned was gone.

I was still in shock when a little gray-haired lady stopped me in the hallway of the guest house where we were staying. She asked me if I was the lady who had lost her home in the fire, and I answered that I was.

"I know just how you feel," she said.

I smiled and mumbled something appropriate, but in my mind I was screaming, *How could you possibly know how I feel? I've just lost everything!*

Then she told me, "One time my house burned down, too." She went on to explain that she was a Jew who had lived in Germany during the Nazi reign of terror. She told me about the terrible night the soldiers had come and forced her family out of their home. "They threw my husband's piano out the window, and it crashed in the street below," she said. "Then they set our house on fire. We stood on the sidewalk and watched it burn."

I stood transfixed as she told how her husband and her six-year-old son were herded onto one truck, while she and her four-year-old daughter were dragged onto another one. As the truck she was in began to move, a guard who had been fingering her little girl's long blonde curls grabbed the child and pulled her off the truck. "I never saw any of my family again," she said. "They all died in the concentration camps."

Then she reached out and gave me a hug. "I know how you feel," she told me. "But in the end you'll find that all those lost things don't matter so much, for no one can ever take away what is locked in your heart."

She was right. The day will come when we will be separated from every single bit of our earthly wealth. But it won't be important. The wealth that really matters is what God has prepared for those who love him.

***

Prayer for Today:
Take my eyes off the things of this world and put them on the eternal things that will never pass away.

Happily Every After

I make known the end from the beginning, from ancient times, what is still to come.

ISAIAH 46:10

"What happened, Grandma? Did they all live happily ever after?"

Aren't happy endings nice? If we had our way, all our stories would end with "happily ever after."

It's the same with life. We want everything to be tied up with neat little bows. If we can't see the resolution, we are restless and uncomfortable.

The thing about the end is that we won't get there until it really is the end. Just look at the story of Moses. Would baby Moses survive his trip down the Nile? Yes ... [happy ending] ... but ... [uh-oh]. Would grown up Moses be able to get Pharaoh to let God's people march away from Egypt and leave their bonds of slavery behind? Yes ... [happy ending] ... but ... [uh-oh]. Would the people be able to make it across the Red Sea without drowning? Yes ... [happy ending] ... but ... [uh-oh]. Would Moses ever step foot onto the Promised Land that flowed with milk and honey? No ... [Awww] ... but ... [oh?].

Actually, the entire Bible is just one long story. We see it begin in the very first verse—(Gn 1:1) "In the beginning God created the heavens and the earth" —and it continues on until the end: "Even so, Lord Jesus, come quickly" (Rv 22:20).

Yes, there will be a happy ending. When Jesus returns to

redeem creation, he will not only make all things right, but he will ensure that they will stay that way forever and ever.

As we see the same mistakes being made today that people have made again and again throughout history, it begins to seem as though life on earth is going round and round in endless circles. No, it is not going in circles. It is moving along page after page. Yes, there will be an ending. And, yes, it will be a happy one.

In the end we'll live happily ever after.

Prayer for Today:
How wonderful it is to know that the end is no mystery to you,
O God. Thank you for the assurance that we will live happily
ever after.